Walking the Talk

Putting Theory into Practice

Twenty-five Narratives from a Faculty of Education

Warnie Richardson
& Carole Richardson

Walking the Talk: Putting Theory Into Practice

Library and Archives Canada Cataloging in Publication

Walking the talk : putting theory into practice / [edited by] Warnie Richardson and Carole Richardson.

ISBN 978-1-55059-361-7

1. Teaching. 2. Teaching--Philosophy. 3. Education--Aims and objectives. I. Richardson, Warnie, 1957- II. Richardson, Carole III. Title.

LB14.7.W3545 2008 370.1 C2008-905977-8

Detselig Enterprises Ltd.
210 1220 Kensington Rd NW
Calgary, Alberta T2N 3P5
www.temerondetselig.com
temeron@telusplanet.net
p. 403-283-0900 *f.* 403-283-6947

We recognize the support of the Government of Canada through the Book Publishing Industry Development Program (BPIDP) for our publishing program.

We also acknowledge the support of the Alberta Foundation for the Arts for our publishing program.

Alberta Foundation for the Arts

SAN 113-0234
ISBN 978-1-55059-361-7
Printed in Canada

Cover Design by James Dangerous

Dedication

To all of our past teachers from Dr. S.E. McDowell Elementary School and Pontiac Protestant High School in Shawville, Quebec who made such a difference in our lives.

We thank you.

Warnie & Carole Richardson

Table of Contents

Foreword

IT IS MY DISTINCT PLEASURE to be asked to write the foreword for this book. As Nipissing University prepares to celebrate 100 years of teacher education, it is fitting that this book brings together the diverse perspectives of twenty-five professors who teach or have taught in our Faculty of Education; a Faculty that graduates over 700 new teachers every year.

The North Bay Normal School opened its doors in 1909, later became the North Bay Teachers' College, and thrives today as the Faculty of Education. With this proud history, the 2009/2010 school year will mark the one hundredth anniversary of preservice education at Nipissing University.

In this book, using specific courses and personal reflections as springboards for discussion, individual professors explore what it means to teach and learn with preservice teachers in a dynamic, cutting edge university environment. They speak with candour of the experiences that have shaped their philosophies and practice, and share that which they consider to be paramount in the education of future teachers.

I'm sure you'll share my view that the conversations, speeches, and narratives in this book provide key insights into teaching and learning, and offer valuable lessons to preservice teachers, preservice educators, and teachers in the field.

Dr. Dennis Mock
President, Nipissing University

Introduction

THE IDEA FOR THIS BOOK had its genesis at a faculty Christmas gathering several years ago. Late into the evening, the conversation, as it had on many previous social occasions, eventually turned to matters of work. As per usual, Ministerial directives were discussed, matters pertaining to university affairs were discussed, the latest research in our respective fields was certainly discussed, but gradually the conversation (as it usually had the habit of doing) morphed into something far more individual, and certainly far more personal. Without fail, when professors from Nipissing's Faculty of Education traditionally gather, the conversation inevitably turns to the collective lament that has each of us, within our individual disciplines, weighing that delicate balance between the material we feel we should incorporate into our courses and teach and the very few hours that have been provided to us for the purposes of accomplishing this task. The one difference on this particular occasion, however, was that the gathering was held at our house, and as hosts, we circulated and found ourselves listening very attentively to the opinions of all of our guests. We remember it as an incredibly impassioned, intelligent discussion, with all of our friends from the Maths, Sciences, Arts, Humanities, Curriculum Development, Language and Literacy, Management, Special Education, Educational Psychology, and Education and Schooling domains, very effectively articulating how, despite many constraints, chief among them time, they worked to ensure their courses met the needs of the greatest majority of their students. At the end of the evening, and after a long night of informal but quite remarkable conversation, the vision of a book inspired by these conversations began to take shape.

To see if we were alone in our assessment of the evening's conversation, early in the New Year we decided to send out a faculty-wide call for essays, open to each one of our colleagues, which would invite them to address, in narrative form, the following general question. With the limited number of teaching hours within your various disciplines, and given the delicate balance between Ministry dictum, text book theory, and practical application, what is/are the most important thing(s) – key understandings, knowledge, skills, and values – that you want your preservice teachers to take away from your course? We stressed that this was not intended to be a research paper or an "official" course outline; instead, we made it very clear that the intent of the project was to have each participant describe their course from a very personal perspective, and in a very informal way. We suggested that they might consider commenting on how, what, and why they choose to prioritize different areas, and how they balance philosophy, theory, and content with the more practical aspects of the profession.

To better illustrate to our colleagues the essence of what it was we were looking for in this proposed literary effort, we used Special Education/Educational Psychology and Music as prototypes, claiming that if all eight professors at Nipissing within those particular disciplines submitted pieces addressing the book's general question, there was a strong likelihood that they would all look dramatically different (at least this is what we initially thought). By way of example, we suggested that within the teaching of Special Education and Educational Psychology, some might see it (as a teaching priority to preservice teachers) as lying beyond Skinner; beyond Erickson; beyond Bandura; beyond constructivism, behaviorism, and humanism; beyond the intricacies of fetal alcohol spectrum disorder and "the new morbidity"; even beyond specific governmental regulation, lying somewhere instead in that very practical and all quite visible area that – although hard to describe and even harder to measure – nevertheless distinguishes some "special" educators as being truly exceptional. In Music Education, we suggested that the approaches might differ according to instrumental/choral/general specialties, all, of course, irrevocably shaped by personal and professional narratives within the music domain. We suspected that although perspectives might prove to be incredibly varied, they should, nevertheless, prove to be very informative, and indeed, at least in our view, most interesting.

For many educators, articulating what one considers to be the essence of what one teaches is sometimes difficult. The word 'curriculum' often comes to mind, but is usually offered with a number of qualifiers. An individual's perception of the concept of curriculum is influenced by one's personal philosophy, psychology, sociology, and history, as these are essentially the foundations of curriculum. Throughout the exploration of development, implementation, evaluation, assessment, and personal understanding, consensus on the specificities of curriculum continues to be elusive. Definitions from authors in the field range from "all the experiences a learner has under the guidance of the school" (Foshay cited in Connelly and Clandinin, 1988, p.5), to "Curriculum is a moving form" (Grumet cited in Gallagher, 2000, p.119). For many studying in and writing about the field of curriculum, attempts to define and develop curriculum have given way to the need to understand curriculum as experience and interaction, rather than a syllabus or subject matter (Conle, 1998). Connelly and Clandinin believe that "it is teachers' 'personal knowledge' that determines all matters of significance relative to the planned conduct of classrooms" (1990, p.4).

Within these pages, the stories told by these preservice educators invite us to understand the impact that personal knowledge has on what we teach, and why we teach the way we do. As stories of professional practice and personal experience intertwine with the questions we continue to ask of ourselves and of our students, one question in particular is highlighted again and again. How does our life experience continue to shape who we are as teachers? We believe that, in the stories that follow, this vitally important question is addressed sometimes implicitly, sometimes explicitly, but always honestly and passionately by twenty-five experienced and dedicated educators.

References

Connelly, F. M., & Clandinin, D. J. (1990). Stories of experience and narrative inquiry. *Educational Researcher*, 19(5), 2-14.

Connelly, F. M., & Clandinin, D. J. (1988). *Teachers as curriculum planners: Narratives of experience.* New York: Teachers College Press.

Conle, C. (1998, September). *A narrative curriculum in teacher education*. A paper delivered at Charles University in Prague, Czech Republic. Retrieved May 23, 2001, from http://www.pedf.cuni.cz/svi/vydavatelstvi/ucitel/ref/conle.html

Gallagher, K. (2000). *Drama education in the lives of girls.* Toronto, ON: University of Toronto Press.

Real Teachers Don't Teach Subjects

Jennifer Barnett

VISIONS OF *LITTLE HOUSE ON THE PRAIRIE*, *Kindergarten Cop*, or *Dangerous Minds* echo in the minds of many preservice candidates. Remembering back to their own school days, they recollect exciting subjects, wonderful teachers, and funny situations. Many of their anecdotes centre on misbehaviors they witnessed, participated in, or devised. In preparation for encountering similar situations, they eagerly await exposure to the quick fix.

In practicum, these beginning teachers may witness an amazing teacher with excellent control utilize a management technique. They become disheartened when they take the technique, apply it in the classroom, and have it fail. Having a preconceived notion of a skills list – which, when executed, will quickly remedy any situation – some students become disillusioned when an apparent answer is not immediately forthcoming. The reality is that if such a quick fix did exist, many of the behavioral situations remembered from their own educational experience would not have occurred. There is no simple solution that will work with every discipline problem. A strategy or technique is useless if the teacher does not understand students, understand themselves, and has not been proactive from the beginning of the year.

Just as a child's behavior cannot fit neatly into a package, so managing children in a classroom cannot be easily wrapped and presented. This is why teachers who have excellent classroom management are often referred to as gifted teachers. These strong classroom managers recognize that misbehaviors are not the result of any deep-rooted deficiency within the student. They are not the fault of a flaw in personality or a poor home environment. Good managers place these common misbehaviors in perspective, making it easier to deal with these situations with consistency, patience, and professionalism.

Teachers don't teach subjects. They don't teach grades. They teach children. Children are individuals with their own understandings, expectations, needs, reactions, and background experiences. Further, as human beings, children are naturally social creatures. Humans live in communities and group together in family units. Social interaction is such a part of our natural make-up that we recognize specific people in our lives before we eat solid food. We begin to learn how to communicate before we walk. Therefore, it is understandable that a group of individuals of a similar age placed together will naturally seek entertainment through social interaction. For this reason, there have always been management problems in schools. Misbehaviors are the natural result of grouping social beings together.

Acknowledging this, the proactive teacher knows classroom management begins before the first child even enters the classroom. By decorating the classroom with relevant subject material and including locations for class work, they personalize the room for the students. Students are less likely to destroy what is theirs. They arrange the classroom so that high traffic areas are free of distraction while ensuring that they can see every child. They visit previous teachers to find out which students work well together and which students may need to be situated separately. In order to prevent future disruptionsThey arrange the desks so that left-handed and right-handed students who sit together will not be bumping elbows. They recognize assigning names to coat hooks and to boot racks may alleviate future arguments. While all of these issues seem minor, many classroom discipline issues stem from negligible irritants which could easily have been prevented.

As beginning teachers often lack confidence in their own abilities, they can misinterpret misbehavior as a reflection on personal competency. As a result, they begin to place a great deal of importance on having the students *like* them. In doing so, they are attempting to meet their own needs, not the needs of the students. The students in turn come to realize that the teacher can be manipulated. This eventually leads to discipline problems in the classroom.

Respect and fondness stems from student recognition of an honest, caring, and trustworthy authority figure. A strict disciplinarian, a gentle student-centred teacher, and an active teacher who focuses on co-operative learning can all be respected and liked by their pupils. Students appreciate a teacher who is consistent and will follow up unfailingly with appropriate consequences. In order to insure that the teacher is as he or she appears, students test expectations. Testing is the students' natural way of ensuring that the teacher is honest, trustworthy, and sincere.

It is next to impossible to provide structure and consistency in a classroom if the teacher is unaware of his/her own boundaries. Teaching is a profession because it involves more then the distribution of subject knowledge and the regurgitation of facts. Teaching is a profession because it promotes understanding of the world and understanding of self. We want students to become contributing members of society while remaining loyal to their own individuality and beliefs. It is then logical to assume that this is also what we must expect of our teachers. If a teacher does not truly value what he or she says, the students will know. Further, they will see the teacher as dishonest, and therefore not deserving of respect. Teachers need to seek to understand where the 'line' is for them. They need to understand which behaviors they will ignore and deal with later and which require immediate attention. What is a 'big deal' for one teacher may be 'trivial' for another. It is vital that new teachers listen to what their conscience is attempting to tell them. Acquiring this understanding of self and professional boundaries is not an simple task, especially for those new to the profession. It is easy to get caught up in the time demands of the job and forget the personal requirement of 'me time'. Time for self and involvement in outside activities give life purpose, and are vital to securing strong mental health. Mental health provides the strength to support decisions when attempting to come to terms with professional management boundaries.

No list of skills or amount of training in implementation can equal a teacher who truly seeks to provide consistency and trust within the classroom. There is no lesson plan for management. There is no clear set of rules. Rooted in understanding of self and students, classroom management comes from within the professional teacher.

Let Me Tell You a Story. . .

Dean B. Berry

"BEGIN AT THE BEGINNING!" a colleague said when I agonized over the fact that I was not happy with my contribution to this text. "Tell them about how you arrived where you are as a university professor teaching language and literacy to preservice teachers. Tell them the most important things you want them to take away from your course." That's a very tall order, I thought. I teach a foundation course on Language and Literacy, and I always begin the year with a story. So let me tell you a story, the same Literacy Soul Story I share with my preservice teachers at the beginning of each year. The same assignment I ask them to do for their first language and literacy class. I ask them to tell me their Literacy Soul Story. I tell them they can use any medium they choose – written text, CD, sculpture, oil painting, video – anything that reflects their story. I feel strongly that this kind of reflective assignment will get them in touch with their own literacy development and will impact on how they will teach literacy.

What has this got to do with my teaching philosophy? It has everything to do with how I developed my teaching philosophy. It has everything to do with walking the talk. On the first day of class, I share my Literacy Soul Story written on a cracked floor tile. I framed it to keep the pieces in place. I show the students the tile as I begin to read aloud from the broken tile pieces.

❧MY LITERACY SOUL STORY❧ I didn't read as a young child. Reading was a puzzle to me. I couldn't put the pieces together. In fact, I couldn't really read until I was eight or nine. I was a struggling reader, dare I say a broken reader like this tile, all the way through school. I was one of those high school struggling readers. I am dyslexic. I only became an adult reader by chance when I was about eighteen or nineteen. But let's get on with the story.

I avoided reading in school, and most certainly out of school. The worst present anyone could give me was a book; so they didn't. A misguided relative would occasionally make that mistake, but the book would gather dust on a shelf somewhere, unopened and untouched. I have no memories of my mother or father reading to me, or of living in a house full of books. I have no memories of going to the library with my family. It wasn't that my parents couldn't read. Both were high school graduates, and my mother was a college graduate. They read the newspaper regularly. It just never occurred to them that it was important to read bedtime storybooks to their children.

Because I come from a large extended family, I was lucky to have many other adults in my life. I used to regularly visit with my great aunt Edith, or "Dede". She assumed the role of a very significant adult in my early life, a grandmother figure. Before I was five, and not yet in school, I spent lots of time in her company. She was a passionate reader who read aloud to me. She read lots and lots of stories to me. To this day, I have fond memories of snuggling down in bed with her to listen to bedtime stories, or of snuggling up on the sofa on a rainy day to listen to stories.

As a result of these early "read-alouds", I was told that my expectations of becoming a reader were very high when I began school at age six. In fact, I fully expected to learn to read the first day. After all, my Aunt Dede said I would learn to read when I went to school, and she would not lie to me.

My mother recounts that when I did not learn to read in the first week of school, I packed up all my little golden picture books, presents from my great aunt Dede, and put them at the back of my clothes closet! As far as anyone can recall, I never took them out again. I had been betrayed; I had not learned to read when I went to school like everyone had told me!

As my grade one year progressed, all the children around me were learning to read, but I was not. I remember the panic of knowing I would be asked to read from the big Dick and Jane book which Mrs. Mclean had up at the front of the class. No matter how hard I tried, I could not make out what the black marks said. When my turn came around, I started to cry, and was passed over. This was the beginning of my elaborate avoidance strategies towards reading in class, and reading at all!

I credit my great aunt with keeping literacy alive for me during my elementary school years. Dede was an avid reader herself, and made frequent trips to the library. It never occurred to her that a seven or eight year old would not want to go to a library. So whenever I visited her in Montreal during school holidays, we made a trip to the library. I was deposited in the Westmount Public Library children's section as she looked for her books. I looked at the picture books and magazines to pass the time. It seemed an age before Dede emerged from behind the stack of book shelves to inquire what I had chosen. I'd mutter I couldn't decide. She would then take a children's book down off the shelf; usually a book she spotted as one she had remembered. She just knew I would love to hear it! She was well aware that I couldn't read it myself. My dearest and clearest memories are of when she read aloud to me from the Burgess Bedtime Stories. *I remember how I felt next to her on the couch, the way she peered thorough top of her reading glasses, but most of all, her voice. Nearly fifty years later, I can still hear exactly how she sounded. That voice was everything for me. I remember that she read aloud all the fairytales, everything Beatrix Potter ever wrote, and a chapter book called* Rebecca of Sunnybrook Farm *which I adored. I first met Ratty and Toad through her readings. The Brothers Grimm became good friends, despite their scary stories. To this day, I love being read aloud to! Each read-aloud gave me the dazzling richness of new worlds: real or imaginary. I now realize this was the lasting gift of literacy I got from her. Listening to read-alouds is an essential component for young children's emergent reading development. But I digress from my story.*

In my six-going-on-seven-year-old mind, reading became something that other children could do effortlessly, but not me. Reading became associated with the drill and workbook pages from the Dick and Jane series. I could not do it. I became very slow and precise in my printing; super neat in order to avoid having to finish the page. It worked! Dawdle a lot, be nice and neat, erase a lot, and you end up never finishing a page of any workbook. The pay off? You save face. You save facing the red marks on the page and lots of corrections. You just did not finish, and often, if you were lucky, the teacher would just let it go and move on. Few teachers ever knew I could not do the work in the first place; I was just a slow poke.

These strategies were useful up until grade three. By this time I had learned to read a little bit. I was in the lowest reading group. I felt like a dummy. In fact, I knew I was a dumb, because I couldn't read like the others in the class.

The crunch came in grade four, with the geography text. The first unit was on the Belgium Congo, about the life of a little boy called Bunga. How do I remember all this? Because my best friend Barbara was a super reader, and told me all about the chapter on our twenty-minute walk to school. She became, unknowingly, my reader/informant. Like all good readers, she wanted to share and discuss what she had read with someone. With very little coaxing from me, Barbara would tell me about any homework reading assignment we had during our walk to school. All I had to do was to ask her what she thought about . . . ? She was off, giving me a running account of the text! I developed an excellent auditory memory and superior listening skills, which would both prove to be good non-reading survival strategies.

These strategies proved extremely useful throughout high school as all good readers, by inclination, love to be asked their opinion of texts! Throughout high school, I managed to get away with only reading bits of assignments and texts. I never completed a novel. I learned to stay after school to ask the teacher to go over the assignments again, that is, read it to me, and explain orally what I had to do. My mother or Barbara became my editors whenever I had to hand in any writing.

As a dysfunctional reader and writer, it took me twice as long to complete anything. Endless writing and rewriting took inordinate amounts of time, as this was pre-word processor times. I regularly did very poorly on exams, since I couldn't write my ideas down coherently on paper within the three-hour exam period. There were no accommodations for special needs learners in those days! In those days, one could attend summer school and rewrite exams in August, and then pass on to the next grade. So I went to school year round, regularly attending summer school as other teenagers my age were working summer jobs.

How did I finally learn to become "a reader"? It was by pure chance, due to another significant adult in my life. My favourite uncle Jack, who was an avid reader, had an accident. He landed in bed, incapacitated with two broken legs. My aunt needed help with my three young cousins, so I moved in with them for about ten months. They had a house full of books, and were both avid readers. They read bedtime stories to their children every night, and often asked me to fill in with this activity. I could handle reading the picture books, but not the chapter books very well, especially not reading aloud in the characters' voices!

My uncle's friends arrived regularly with books, which he devoured rapidly. His sick room was overflowing with all kinds of books, and like all readers, he liked to talk about what he was reading. He would suggest I read such and such a book because . . . giving me personal commercials about the book. At eighteen, I was too embarrassed to say I did not read for fun, so I would take the Agatha Christie mystery he raved about and wade my way through it to please him. He invited a reader's response from me about the parts I liked best, the characters, or what I thought about the clever way the author had developed the plot. He was the first adult who told me it was not necessary to read every word in a text. It was okay to skip the boring parts of a description, he said and get on with the plotline if I wanted. This is a skill, and a message I had never heard as a struggling reader. He also said if I did not like a book, it was all right to stop reading and abandon it. There was no rule, he said, that I had to finish every book I started! However, we did talk about why I didn't like the book whenever this happened.

He asked me about my opinion on the author's style and voice; something of which I had been totally unaware. He talked about carrying on conversations with authors (a completely new idea to me). I soon found that each writer gave me the dazzling richness of their worlds: real or imaginary. This is what my great Aunt Dede had done for me with her read-alouds. I began to revel in the invented kingdoms of authors for myself. As a child, I had not learned that I could engage with this magical aspect of reading. I had not learned all through school that two quite different sources of information are involved in the reading process, one source being the author who provides the ink marks or visual information, and the other source the reader herself, who provides the non-visual information. Up to this time, I had never been really engaged in the reading process!

My uncle unknowingly gave me another gift of literacy. Through his gentle coaxing, I learned to choose my own books and to view reading with excitement and passion. I learned to see reading as a transactional process. I began to view reading not as a passive activity, but a very active invisible activity of the mind. I began to see that literacy "has more to do with the delights than the mechanics of reading. It is not a skill acquired once in a lifetime, but an art to be practiced and polished one's whole life" (Keefer 1990 p.121).

Later, as a newly minted novice elementary teacher, I met children in my classes who – like myself at their age – were not engaged in reading. They had no idea what reading was about. For them, learning to read was the basal reader and the drudgery of workbook pages, and endless drills on nonsensical sound-symbols. These standardized controlled vocabulary reading programs certainly were never a joy to teach. I could see how humiliating and painful the lessons were for these struggling readers; they wanted to avoid these lessons, as I had done. They felt stupid compared to their peers, just as I had. They quickly became demoralized, and refused to try any longer. It was just not worth their risking their self esteem. I recognized their anxieties, as well as their avoidance techniques. I knew the basal reader had not made me a reader, and it was not going to make them readers either.

My uncle had made me a reader, but how and why did this happen?

I went back to graduate school to become a literacy educator, and to find out what I could do to help struggling readers bridge their literacy gaps. One of the first courses I took was on children's literature. It opened up a new world to me. As an adult, I learned for the first time what I had missed during all those years of non-reading! I discovered whole genres of children's stories through Sheila Egoff's work. While my fellow students were rereading their childhood favourites, I was reading children's books for the first time. I realized that engaging with books, sharing them, talking about them, and reading them out aloud was a huge component in the teaching of reading. I had forgotten my own experience with my great aunt and uncle. I should have been using real books in my classroom with those struggling readers. I should have been using read-alouds of all kinds! I had forgotten how important it was for developing readers to talk, to discuss, or to argue passionately about the stories they read or hear together.

If you decide to teach by walking the talk, a classroom has to become a safe learning environment, a learning group in fact. Using the Literacy Soul Stories as a starter activity helps to bring this about. Every year there are some students who, like me, remember not being successful readers in school. When they share their Literacy

Soul Stories with their classmates, it is often the first time they are willing to risk telling their peers of their own struggles. I encourage my preservice teachers to share their Literacy Soul Stories with their future classes, so that their students will view them as authentic people, and later as authentic teachers.

As a university literacy teacher educator, I realized that I had to do more than lecture to my preservice teachers about the teaching of literacy, I had to involve them. I had to walk the talk and demonstrate strategies they could use. As a result, I now encourage them to learn all they can about children's literature; to explore a wide variety of genres so that they will be able to lure all their readers into the readers' club. I demonstrate reading aloud in our first class, so that they will learn to read some story that speaks to them with passion and excitement. I tell them why a piece of fiction or non-fiction spoke to me. I invite them to respond. Then I invite each preservice teacher to sign up to practice reading aloud once in our Language and Literacy class. Some are reluctant to read aloud during the first term, as they see no point to this kind of "flakey" university activity. However, by the beginning of the second term, the requests for repeat read alouds start to flood in as they just have to share this neat book or article they found with our class! They just know the rest of our class members need to hear about this article, story or book. It sometimes requires creative scheduling to keep up with the requests! But more importantly, it does tell me that the learning environment has become a risk-free one for them. We are becoming a learning community. It does tell me that they are becoming passionate about literacy!

It is essential that preservice teachers understand that children of all ages need to be read aloud to on a regular basis, not only at home, but also at school. We should start with short periods of time, then gradually increase the read aloud times, Jim Trelease says in his marvellous book for parents and teachers. All children need to be provided with a wide variety of printed materials, and be encouraged to explore them, which is why all my preservice teachers are invited to develop their read aloud skills. They begin to realize that these read aloud activities are strategies to help teach the foundations of literacy of which Holdaway writes so eloquently. Once the concept of story has been acquired, the child can and will attend to the mechanics of reading, but not before. Older students need to be read to daily too. It only takes a few weeks of ten minute read alouds for my university preservice students to become hooked. So I actively encourage the future high school preservice teachers to take the time to read aloud in their subject classes. By doing so, they can hook their students into the worlds of the historian, geographer, scientist, mathematician. It is the teacher's job to find just the right book/article for that particular young adult. What young adult can resist a teacher who approaches them with a text saying, "I saw this article and thought of you" or "I thought of you when I came across this book"? These are critical messages for preservice student teachers to give, and to understand the impact they can make on a student. Many preservice students lack this understanding when they arrive in my university classroom.

Preservice teachers need to recognize that, for some children, learning to read is more difficult than it is for others. They need more nurturing and attention in school from a skilled and insightful teacher, a mentor who will enhance their self esteem. It is the literacy teacher's job to find just the right book for that particular child or young adult to lure them towards books. These children are not dim-witted and unable to learn, as I have heard exasperated teachers moan in staffroom chatter. I firmly believe that the reading process is the same complex task for all human beings. However it takes more time and energy for some of us to learn. As teachers, we often give up too soon or get sidetracked by focusing on only one or two aspects of the reading process, hence sacrificing the student's self-worth. We also sacrifice the books and the invented kingdoms of authors! We spend too much time on the black ink marks or visual information on the page and the skill aspects of reading, and neglect to involve the student with the glorious non-visual aspects of reading. Preservice teachers need to understand that of course, everyone should be able to handle the grapho-phonic symbols of printed text but, despite the cries of some, literacy is much more than this. It is more than the ability to read signs, bank statements, newspapers, magazines. Too often in discussions with preservice teachers, it is only the mechanics of reading that is thought of as being important. If they continue to hold on to this idea they, in turn, will pass on this misconception to children and to parents, so that the public at large will continue to believe it as well.

There are numerous studies cited in *Becoming a Nation of Readers* that show that the amount of time spent on actual reading in the regular classroom is very little, and even less in the special education classrooms, where the struggling readers are imprisoned!

Many teachers do not want to waste time on reading books. They prefer instead to spend time on what is referred to as "direct teaching", the teaching of the mechanics of the reading system. The truly critical aspects of literacy never get addressed. Preservice teachers need to realize that literacy teaching is a lot like medicine. If you don't diagnose the problem correctly, the student may never visit the wonderful invented worlds of authors. Could that be considered a chronic illness of the imagination?

Preservice teachers need to understand that literacy means different things to different people. First, there is the kind of literacy which requires only the reading of a few signs, numbers, or words within the environment. This limited type of literacy really results in a person being cut off from the verbal world. These readers are cut off from everything that requires verbal understanding. They are outside the "literacy club" that Frank Smith talks and writes of so eloquently.

The second kind of literacy involves the person reading and writing sufficiently to carry out their job. That is, they can read the technical reports, newspapers, magazines, and anything practical that concerns them. They don't read for pleasure. Reading is not a part of their non-work related activities. For these individuals, reading never becomes an entrancing experience.

This is true for many students who graduate from schools, colleges, and universities. I meet these preservice student teachers every September when they enter our faculty of education to become teachers. They have an image of themselves as subject area specialists. They are going to be a Social Studies or Science teacher, and it is this content that they are going to teach their students.

These preservice teachers need to learn to teach their subject specialty with a view of literacy as an extension of a person's language usage and personal knowledge. To paraphrase Robertson Davies, this kind of literacy involves reading to ask questions, to explore thinking, and to enlarge the reader's knowledge. This type of literacy is the ability to stand on another's shoulders, to see the things that have lifted us out of the mud further and clearer, with splendor and beauty. It is what Robert MacNeil talks of in his book *Wordstruck* as a place to escape to with your spirit where words can make another place. He describes this as a blissful experience. Even content area specialists need to teach towards this blissful experience.

One of the major goals of literacy has always been to move closer to what is true, regardless of cultural boundaries. And almost always, the truth is something other than what we might have wanted it to be. The truth of this can be seen in the research on how best to teach literacy. Few spheres of education have generated more research or controversy. Perhaps this is why there has been so much resistance and misunderstanding about the seminal literacy research of Adams, Chall, Cay, Booth, Wells, Goodman, Graves, Calkins, and others; not to mention the banning of some reading programs despite having been developed upon a sound and rich research foundation. It has given rise to the "never ending debate" says Smith. This sidetracks us from another goal of literacy: to develop our facility for language by introducing us to the greatest minds of times past. Words can reach across time and space. Reading can put us in communication with others' ideas and thoughts.

So with this in mind, my preservice teachers are asked to do some research on a teaching strategy that they can use in their classroom. They are asked to find out what the latest literacy research says and to be ready to defend it in class. Why? Because they need to be knowledgeable about research, and to be able to defend or support a choice of literacy strategy to their future principal or to a parent of their future students.

They are always surprised at the amount of research on literacy and how best to teach it. Many had no idea that literacy teaching could be so political and polarizing. The "never ending debate" continues. We bring the debates into the university classroom as these students are encouraged to share their findings.

All children, and my preservice students included, need to be praised for their efforts at reading and writing. All children need to have paper, pencils, markers, and crayons readily available. Children need to dictate their first stories and have them displayed. In short, my preservice teachers will meet children, regardless of their age, who come to school without a rich literacy background and need unlimited opportunities for reading and writing. Such programs take time, and teachers, as well as parents, need to recognize that this is time well spent. So despite being a university classroom, my classroom reflects this, and has plastic bins of such materials available to all. My preservice students are encouraged to write daily in class then talk and share their efforts. The university classroom bulletin boards display their first writing drafts of stories and poems. Their research class assignment on a teaching strategy becomes a published work for others and all are shared on a CD at the end of the course. There is a purpose to and for their writing. It is for their peers to read. For some of my preservice students, this represents the first time anyone has asked them to share their writing in a meaningful way. It is sometimes the first time they have ever been asked to write and read to publication standards. It is gratifying to hear from former students, now teachers, who email with me the news that they have just published their first book of stories or poetry. They developed enough courage to venture out and write on their own, because they first shared their writing in our university class,

It is a tragedy when statistics show us that far too many children and adults are never entranced by reading. Many of my preservice students read functionally, but never in their lives stumble upon the bliss of reading as I did. To lure them into involvement with books, I encourage them to look at the work of researchers such as Daniels, Cunningham, and Allington, then to choose a novel, a story, that speaks to them. I ask them to find three other classmates who feel the same and develop a four-six week curriculum literature unit around the novel together. They will introduce the novel to us in an interactive workshop format. They will, in other words, have to "sell" us on the idea of using their book choice in a classroom. They need to tell us all about the kinds of interesting cross-curriculum activities that this novel stimulates. They will need to develop activities that a variety of learners can participate in. Their unit will be published and shared with the rest of the class. I tell them that I expect controversy in their presentation, debates, and passion. They are not to lecture us, they are to engage us.

So what is the most important thing I want my preservice teachers to take away from my course? I want my preservice teachers to become knowledgeable teachers of reading and writing with a passion for their subject and a passionate desire to teach it to others. I truly believe it is never too late and the student is never too old to become a passionate reader and, in turn, a passionate teacher. It has to be nurtured by educators who are passionate about teaching themselves.

In the same way that a "reader" or a "writer" is not born but has to be nurtured by educators who are readers and writers themselves, I firmly believe that the desire to teach is rarely born and must be nurtured. I walk the talk with my preservice teachers. Discussion is not enough. I have to demonstrate that enthusiasm, love of books, and writing is contagious. I have to demonstrate to them that so much of the success in helping youngsters become readers and writers will depend not so much on the technical skills, but upon the passion they communicate as teachers of their subject. And so I urge future teachers to start their daily lessons passionately, with the irresistible invitation in the words, "Let me tell you a story . . . "

References

Adams, Marilyn Jagger. 1990. *Beginning to Read: Thinking and Learning About Print*. Cambridge, Mass.: The MIT Press.

Anderson, Richardson C., Elfrieda H. Hiebert, Judith Scott, and Ian A.G. Wilkinson. 1985. *Becoming A Nation of Readers*. Champaign-Urbana, IL: Center for the Study of Reading.

Booth, David. 1989. Keynote address. Child-Centred Experience-Based Learning Conference. Winnipeg, Manitoba. February.

Calkins, Lucy McCormick. 1991. *Living Between the Lines*. Portsmouth, NH: Heinemann.

Chall, J.S. 1989. Learning to read: The great debate twenty years later. A response to "Debunking the great phonics myth". *Phi Delta Kappan*, 71,521-538.

Clay, Marie M. 1991. *Becoming Literate: The Construction of Inner Control*. Portsmouth, NH: Heinemann.

Cunningham, Patricia M. and Allington, Richard L. 1999. *Classrooms That Work, They Can All Read and Write*. Addison -Wesley Educational Publishers.

Daniels, Harvey. 2002. *Literature Circles. Voice and Choice in Book Clubs and Reading Groups*. Portland, Maine: Stenhouse Publishers.

Egoff, Shelia, G. T. Stubbs, and L. F. Ashley. 1969. *Only Connect*. New York: Oxford University Press.

Davies, Robertson. 1990. A Chat About Literacy. *More Than Words Can Say*, Toronto: McClelland and Stewart Inc.

Goodman, Ken. 1986. *What's Whole in Whole Language?* Portsmouth, NH: Heinemann.

Keefer, Janice Kulyk. 1990. Arks and Tunnels. *More Than Words Can Say*, Toronto: McClelland and Stewart Inc.

MacNeil, Robert. 1989. *Wordstruck*. New York: Harper.

Trelease, Jim. 1989. *The New Read-Aloud Handbook*. Penguin Books.

Smith, Frank. 1988. *Joining the Literacy Club*. Portsmouth, NH: Heinemann.

Smith, Frank. 1992. *Learning to Read: The Never-Ending Debate*. Phi Delta Kappan. February, 432-441.

Wells, Gordon. 1986. *The Meaning Makers: Children Learning Language and Using Language to Learn*. Portsmouth, HN: Heinemann.

Teaching Curriculum Studies Music to Primary/ Junior Teacher Candidates

Wynne Blair

When one is hired to teach at a faculty of education, the responsibility of the future generation of teachers can lie heavily upon one's shoulders. Couple this with the fact that most Curriculum Studies courses are a mere twenty-four hours. Now add on the fact that we are a laptop institution. Then you have some understanding of how carefully we need to prioritize what we will teach in terms of key understanding, knowledge, skills, and values.

For me, the most important part of my course rests in the area of values. Since I concur with many others such as Miller, (2001) Davis, (2001), Booth, (2001) Upitis, (2001) and Lewis (2001) that it is every child's right to have a strong arts education in the public school system, my first priority is to convince my students that they will not be one of those teachers that skips music in order to cover the expectations in math, language, and science. Armed with a guided imagery exercise patterned after Ferrucci, (1982) in which we explore the importance of the arts and physical activity for all people, I attempt to lead my students through a process in which they recognize the central role of the arts and physical education in school. After all, is that not what they remember about their primary education all these years later? Were we not happiest when participating in one or more of these specialty subjects, because they matched our own strengths, our strongest of the multiple intelligences? After the guided imagery session, we share a couple of fun musical experiences and use them as the basis to brainstorm why we should teach music. I also summarize my experiences as both a music and kindergarten educator in which children with disabilities and/or emotional problems learned to read through music. This is reinforced with readings by Wilkinson (1999), Reid (1995), Thomas (1996), Smithrim and Upitis (2003), and *The Ontario Curriculum: the Arts* (1998). Most students are surprised to learn that it is actually the law that we teach all subjects, not just those that we feel are necessary or the ones in which we believe we have some talent.

Next, we explore why teachers don't teach music. We begin to understand that in most cases, it is our own fear of incompetence that gets in our way. We create a space in which the education students begin to realize that fear of the unknown is normal, and that when we are afraid, the best solution may be to become aware of the community of professionals that is there to help us in a "persons plus" way of working (Perkins, 1995). As they begin to realize that they may be supported by a music consultant, a specialist in the school, resources at the board's teachers' centre, and/or another teacher with the same grade assignment, attempting to teach music may not be as daunting.

Once the "fear factor" is addressed head on, then we can start to learn strategies that anyone, regardless of ability or disability, talent or lack thereof, can use to teach music. This is when the fun really starts. I want our one or two hour sessions together to be that special break in my students' day. If our class time is filled with learning and fun, then they will experience firsthand the role that it can play in a child's curriculum. When I am choosing resources, I introduce them to the programs with the most user-friendly materials for teachers. I carefully demonstrate that while series are written for the music specialists: *Musicanada* Grades 1-8 (Brooks, P., Kovacs, B., Trotter, M., Sunderland, D., 1982) and *Canada is Music*; others are more useful for the novice: *Music Builders* K-8 and *Teachers' Choice* K-8 (Rinaldo, Grosso and Thorne, 1999).

In addition, I make full use of the relevant technology, from a CD player to the best educational software for primary/junior: Music Ace 1 and 2 (Palmer, 2003). I am careful to demonstrate the correct use of CDs on several occasions, so the students who are reluctant to sing realize that there are many good resources they can use in addition to their own voice. I also demonstrate how PowerPoint, Hyper Studio, Inspiration, and internet websites can be applied to make music concepts more accessible to their learners. This enables our university students who are competent with technology to use this skill to enhance their weaker ones in music.

As one student said to me after teaching a music unit on practicum, "I was so busy 'razzle dazzling' them with the technology, when I presented my Hyper Studio presentation on the Baroque Period that I forgot to be frightened that I was teaching music. When the students learned that they were going to produce their own class Hyper Studio on the Classical Period, and that I would teach them how to import music and make symbols move to the music, they were very eager to begin. I couldn't believe how keen they were to study this 'old fashioned' music".

Another student who claimed she had not sung or had much to do with music since she was labeled a "crow" in the junior choir in grade 5 was terrified when her associate asked her to teach music on her placement. We talked it over and she decided that she could cover many of the grade 4 expectations for reading music notation using Music Ace 1 and 2. The students were entranced, and even wanted to play Music Ace over recess. Their teacher was amazed, as she thought this group hated music. When I probed her to tell me how she had sold her music lessons, she admitted that she decided it had to be fun, and she had to get excited about what they were doing so she could sell it to them. When I heard these comments, I knew I had achieved my main goal with at least two students.

Once most of my students have a positive attitude, and I admit that I cannot turn them all to my way of thinking, we work on teaching strategies and content simultaneously. The content is just the basics: beat, rhythm, pitch, timbre, dynamics, and form. I stress how important it is to use all of the learning modalities when approaching music, visual, auditory, and kinaesthetic. Knowing that children (and many grown ups) "certainly relate music and body movement naturally" Gardner (1983, p.123), kinaesthetic learning is often a good place to start (Schnebly-Black & Moore, 2003) even with adult learners. As we stomp the beat, clap the rhythm, create dances, add tuned and untuned percussion instruments, and learn hand signs and hand jives, we not only awaken our brains as explored by Rauscher, (2002) but begin to realize the value of responding to music with our whole bodies. Given that we use music, PowerPoint, charts, Music Ace 1 and 2 and websites for visual learners; CDs, voice, Music Ace 1 and 2, and numerous instruments for auditory learners, our faculty of education students experience music in many modalities.

Since all class notes, schedules, assignments, and presentations are always on my course website, students with learning exceptionalities have the opportunity to both preview and review the material whenever it is convenient for them. The notes have been constructed in class by having a few students in each section revise the original copy on their laptops. Then the new improved note is uploaded to the web, usually within twenty-four hours.

The website became part of my course when I was a participant in one of the Universal Instructional Design Projects, sponsored by the government's Learning Opportunities Task Force, and headed by Jim Bryson (2002). The fundamental belief behind this project is that "all students regardless of ability or disability should have equal access to material and success in a course regardless of ability or disability". Since this philosophy is in tune with my own, making the changes to my course to make it accessible was very rewarding.

To further model the importance of allowing people to learn in their preferred modality using their strengths, my two major assignments have many choices. I find some students want to build instruments, some want to search out music websites, some want to make manipulatives to teach reading music, and still others want to create music lessons using popular music. When given a wide range of choice, all related to music-making or learning, the students enjoy working on their projects, and produce very high-level work. When they can either create a mini-unit plan as a series of lessons or create a Hyper Studio presentation for a period of music, a social studies theme or music unit, once again their energy is engaged, and they produce very professional products.

In summary, in my opinion it is not so much what we teach but how and why we teach it that has the most impact on future teachers. If they graduate with a positive attitude toward all aspects of the curriculum, especially the arts and practical teaching skills, given a little time they will develop and/or access the curriculum they need to be effective with their students. If they truly believe that all of their future students are different learners, and that part of the responsibility of joining this profession is to discover how and what each child can be taught effectively, then the children in their charge will be able to reach their full potential. That thought brings me great hope for the future of education in general, but especially for arts education.

References

Booth, D. (2001). Arts and education 2000, A window for the future and a renaissance for the information age. *Canadian Music Educator* 42 (3) 23.

Davis, W. (2001). Arts and education 2000, A window for the future and a renaissance for the information age. *Canadian Music Educator* 42 (3) 23.

Bowe, F.G. (2000). *Universal design in education - Teaching nontraditional students*. CT: Bergin and Garvey.

Brooks, P., Kovacs, B., Trotter, M., Sunderland, D. (1982). *Musicanada* 1-8. Toronto: Holt, Rinehart and Winston.

Bryson, J. (2003) *Universal instructional design in postsecondary settings: An implementation guide*. Learning Opportunities Task Force, Ministry of Training, Colleges and Universities, Province of Ontario

Ferrucci, P. (1982). *What we may be*. Los Angeles, CA: J.P. Tarcher, Inc.

Gardner, H. (1983). *Frames of mind, the theory of multiple intelligences*. New York: Basic Books.

Lewis, S. (2001). Arts and education 2000, A window for the future and a renaissance for the information age. Canadian Music Educator 42 (3) 25.

Miller, J. (2001). Arts and education 2000, A window for the future and a renaissance for the information age. *Canadian Music Educator* 42 (3) 22.

Palmer, J. (2003). *Becoming a music ace.* The Recorder, XLV (2) 42-44.

Perkins, D.N. (1995) *Smart schools, Better thinking and learning for every child.* New York: The Free Press.

Rauscher, F. (2002). Music education: A resource for children. *Canadian Music Educator*, 44 (2), 8-12.

Reid, S. (1995). Why teach music. *FWTAO Newsletter*, 15 (2), 12-13.

Rinaldo, V., Grosso, C. and Thorne, M. (1999). *Teachers Choice Grades 1-6.* Hamilton, Ontario: emc notes inc.

Schnebly-Black, J. and Moore, S.F. (2003). *The rhythm inside, Connecting body, mind and spirit through music.* Van Nuys, CA: Alfred Publishing Co.

Smithrin, K. & Upitis, R. (2003). Contaminated by peaceful feelings: The power of music. *Canadian Music Educator*, 44 (3), 12-17.

Sylvester, R. (1994). How emotions affect learning. *Educational Leadership*, 52 (2), 60-65.

Thomas, S. (1996). Music in school: An essential for our children's education. *FWTAO Newsletter*, 15 (2) 8-12

Upitis, R. (2001). Arts and education 2000, A window for the future and a renaissance for the information age. *Canadian Music Educator* 42 (3) 24.

Wilkenson, J. (1999). Literacy through the arts. *The Art Paper 9* (3) 1-3.

www.georgianc.on.ca/student-services/c4a/uid_home.htm accessed December 7, 2004.

Windows of Opportunity

Darlene Brackenreed

As I sit at the desk in my office at home thinking about the articulation of my ideas for this submission, I look out the floor to ceiling window, a window that is so expansive as to allow a view of the cul-de-sac on which I live. The three-year-old twins are playing in front of their house with their dad across the street, and I marvel at the opportunity to observe unbeknownst to anyone.

As I watch the boys play, I think of my growing up years in a small farming community where the adage "it takes a village to raise a child" was practiced without question. Community members were aware of each others' situations, be they good, bad, or indifferent, and whenever a family had difficulty of some sort, the community pulled together to provide support. I once had a funeral director in the nearby city tell me that when they conducted a service for our little community, they knew they would have a huge congregation. Did I mention that our community consisted of thirty-seven town folk with about 400 people in the surrounding farms?

Going back to the window looking out into my urban community of today, I notice the six-year-old sister of the twin boys has come out to play. In the future, if one of these children should experience difficulty in their lives, such as in the form of a learning problem, what will the professionals have to say? Will they investigate the dynamics of a family with twins? Will they question the nurturing skills of the parents, and try to assess whether all children received equal attention, or did the twins grab the lion's share? Will the teachers sigh and lament that there is nothing to be done because after all, how can a teacher overcome all the baggage that these children have brought to school with them? Will the parents feel comfortable going to the school? Will they feel up to the prospect of having to advocate for the rights of each of their children? And how will the difficulties, should they occur, be explained? Will, in fact, the family feel a part of the community of the school, or will they feel alienated and unsupported?

I turn back to my computer, and open the file that contains the outline for the course I teach in Educational Psychology and Special Education. As I skim over it, I think of yesterday, when I bumped into one of my recent graduates from the course. Hugh explained that while he had experienced many "aha" moments during the course, others in the class did not or could not. He went on to say that he felt this was due to the fact that he has been teaching for about fifteen years in places such as Korea, and that the theory we discussed answered many questions about why he believed or did certain things and why other teachers perhaps believed or did otherwise. "But the inexperienced persons you have coming into this course have none of this background, and for them it is simply sink or swim". So I wonder. What can those inexperienced students get out of it? Better still, what do I want the students to walk away with? How will my course influence their thinking and practice should one of these students become the future teacher of one of the children on my street in my community?

I am assigned the task of teaching Educational Psychology, but I also believe in the merits of teachers being capable of articulating the reasons why they believe and act upon certain approaches, and also in being able to answer to and challenge their ways of thinking. Theory provides a solid foundation for this to occur. Would any of us be satisfied with the surgeon who in response to the question, "Why?" says because that is what my friend said to do, or because that is what I read on the internet? I would not. But if Hugh is right, and the majority of the students in my classes on theory do not "get it", what shall I do?

The second half of this particular course focuses on teaching about students with exceptionalities. While I accept that many of my students are verbose in their expressions of distaste for theory, it is alarming to me to learn of the number of relatively young and fresh preservice teachers who clearly tell me that they are teaching subjects such as Math and Science, and will not be teaching, as one student put it, any "drooling students sitting in the corner".

Am I up to this challenge? Will I be able to affect their attitudes and soften their position on the attributes of students? Some days I think not and feel discouraged, but when I look across the street at the twins and see their fresh, eager faces, ready to face the world, excited at the prospects of growing up and going to school, I think of the possibilities that await them. And then it is clear to me once again as to why I am here at my university, committed to the advocacy for the rights of all children and the right to a free and appropriate education. Each of us makes a contribution to the quality of life of other persons. Each of us needs love and attention and respect.

This is what I want my preservice teachers to understand. I want them to be clear about what teaching is and is not, and how their role as a teacher dramatically influences the life of a child, past, present and future. I want the preservice teachers to become part of the community of teachers, but also to become part of a community of caring adults who demonstrate qualities reminiscent of my home community, my growing up years, and the close-knit community of the street where I currently live. In these communities, all people share(d) some level of responsibility for the well-being of our members, especially the children and youth.

For example, if my neighbor should suddenly collapse, I would go to assist him rather than point out that there are many people on my street, and I do not have time to give first aid to all of them, just as Rick Lavoie discusses in his timeless video *Fat City*. Additionally, it is important that I understand my limitations and call for expert assistance in dealing with the situation, and in order to do so I must know how to access services, such as calling 911. When my neighbor returns home, I want to be able to support him and help him to be as successful as possible within my role as a neighbor, as well as to provide support to his family. Knowing my boundaries and expectations as a neighbor will help me to deal with the situation, and to provide an inclusive environment where my neighbor is accepted.

It is an idealistic goal, perhaps, but worthwhile and, to some extent, achievable. It is as worthwhile and achievable a goal in our schools as it is in my neighborhood.

I know that my community is not like all other communities, but we can aspire to have caring, supportive, and inclusive environments in our schools where children and youth will share with teachers and parents in the responsibility of a safe and nurturing environment. What does this have to do with Maslow, Bruner, or Vygotsky? What does this have to do with Individual Education Plans, Transition Plans or diagnostic testing and teaching? That is the connection that I struggle to make every day for my preservice students and inservice teachers.

Getting Up Near the Teacher:

Teaching From Who I Am

Terry Campbell

Gotta get up near the teacher if you can
If you wanna learn anything

— Bob Dylan

I have just finished a storytelling and story writing session with a group of Grade 4/5's in a local school here in North Bay. How did I get here? It was the first time in a while that I have directly taught elementary students; for over six years, I have been teaching preservice teachers in a Bachelor of Education program. Although I have been in and out of classrooms during that period of time, it has been mainly to observe and evaluate student teacher performance. And now, here I was, performing and being observed by a classroom teacher, and a teacher candidate who was there on placement.

"What does it feel like to be back 'in the trenches'?" someone asks. Actually, it feels both familiar and wonderful, after overcoming the initial butterflies always involved in the planning and preparing stages of the teaching process. A better metaphor occurs to me: 'back in the saddle.' The war metaphor implies conflicts and enemies, and that's not what it feels like at all. Back in the saddle, I am going along on a ride with the students, over a sometimes bumpy terrain, surprised by the joys, and challenged by the problems that arise along the way. This is closer to my beliefs about what teaching is all about. What are those beliefs, and how do I go about communicating them to the preservice teachers in my course at the university?

What are my guiding beliefs about teaching?

My approach to the education of teacher candidates is guided by my belief that we teach for best educational practice and not just about best practice. By this, I mean that I think we as teachers are most effective when we are able to create the conditions for learning.

What those conditions are vary according to time, place, and most of all, according to the diverse learners with whom we are interacting. How do I know which conditions to create and when? I try to figure that out through careful listening and observing, and by doing my background homework of research and planning.

As I do my research on various topics and methods of instruction and plan ways to present the material so that it makes sense, I am guided by three over-riding principles: principles that are valuable to me both now as an educator of preservice teachers, and in the past when I was a teacher of elementary students.

First of all, I am teaching for *emotional understanding*. It is on this dimension that the diversity of the learners matters most. Every learner has a unique emotional make-up, and our emotional and spiritual sensibilities strongly affect how, when, and if we can learn. This is one of our most complex challenges as teachers, and it applies whether we are teaching teachers-to-be or young children just learning how to read and write. As a language and literacy teacher who is also a storyteller, I make use of the power of story to assist in this complex endeavour to know my students as well as I can, and to demonstrate to them how vital it is to learn about their students, and teach to and for their hearts as well as their minds.

Secondly, I am teaching for *intellectual awareness*. Because I teach the language arts, one of which is drama, this means conveying my understanding of the best ways to teach children how to read and write and become fully literate beings in our complex world. This teaching includes what we know about effective ways of leading children into literacy, including new ways of taking into account today's new literacies. These literacies involve both the traditional reading and writing of conventional print, as well as media works and technological texts. Teaching the new literacies means teaching for multiple ways of demonstrating one's understanding; for example, speaking, singing, drawing, and presenting through movement, visual arts, and drama. Becoming aware of all of these possible modes of expression is integral to becoming literate today, and today's informed teachers are aware of this.

Thirdly, I am teaching for *professional responsibility*. My role in the teacher education program is to be a role model of professionalism. My role is to demonstrate what professionalism looks and sounds like. This means being fully prepared to present course content in an organized fashion in a variety of ways over time from the easily accessible to the more challenging. It also means teaching from who I am: sharing my passions, talents, and experiences in the classroom and in life in general.

Finally, I believe in showing students what it means to love teaching.

What does 'teaching from who I am' mean? The teacher as reader, speaker (storyteller), listener, writer.

I teach a course entitled Language and Literacy, which includes drama integrated into instruction about how to teach the language arts in K-6 classrooms. The language arts include reading, writing, listening, speaking, viewing, and representing. 'Teaching from who I am' means teaching as a visible and audible reader, writer, listener, speaker, viewer, and representer. I would like to focus on who I am as a reader, speaker, listener, and writer and how that shapes my teaching.

Teacher as reader

Last summer I attended The European Congress on Reading held in Berlin. The keynote speaker from Finland presented research on fostering reading engagement in young learners. One of the key factors she highlighted was the practice of classroom teachers who share their passion for reading. They talk enthusiastically about what they are currently reading, from novels and poems to newspaper articles and information books. They put up school-wide displays of "Books that Changed Our Lives." They encourage reading wide varieties of literature by actively promoting them through exciting introductions and then making the books available in the classroom.

When I reflected on my own practice in my course, I felt fairly sure I shared my passion for children's literature successfully. This occurs as an integral part of the read alouds and storytelling included in every session. The students have commented on my enthusiasm for children's books. After hearing about this Finnish research, this year I made a conscious effort to share my passion in a more personal way, bringing in newspaper articles that had moved me and talking about what novels I was reading, who my favourite authors are, and current articles and informational texts I find interesting. In return, I receive similar communication from my students: they write and tell me about what they are reading and what they find interesting. I've learned about how frustrated they are about the lack of time to engage in 'pleasure reading.' They've also informed me about new authors and about the wide variety of informational sources they use. By speaking about myself as a reader, I was led to listen to them about who they are as readers.

Teacher as speaker (storyteller)

As well as being a voracious reader, I am also a storyteller. This seems to me to be a wonderful ancient art to pass on to the next generation of teachers. I tell stories, and I teach them how to learn a story to tell in the traditional oral fashion. Lately I had begun thinking about how to teach children to be storytellers, and how this might be an effective rehearsal for story writing. That led me to try it out in a real classroom, which is how I ended up in the Grade 4/5 classroom. So far I have taken over their literacy block for three sessions. The students are embracing the storytelling with eagerness, but it will take a little longer to see how this translates into their writing.

When I asked the Grade 4/5 students to talk and write about how storytelling might help their story writing, one student said, "How will blabbing about a story help me to write it?" But he did go on to tell a beautifully shaped story based on *The Name of Tree: A Bantu Tale* (set in central Africa) by changing the setting to the Great Wall of China. It will be interesting to hear their perceptions of whether and how the telling helps the writing after a few more weeks. I'll be anxious to share the results with the preservice teachers.

I am also dedicated to the idea of teaching 'good talk' practices in classrooms. By talking and listening to one another, about a book the group has just read or a film they have seen together, students hone their abilities to articulate their ideas, and to listen to multiple points of view and perspectives. I have written extensively about this elsewhere, as it was my dissertation topic (*Good Talk about Great Literature*), and I try to emphasize the value and importance of promoting rich oral discussions through literature circles and classroom book clubs.

Teacher as listener

There is much made of the fact that students need to listen in order to learn. This includes the obvious behavioral factors that accompany "good listening" in the classroom, as well as the indicators of effective listening for learning, which are closely aligned with comprehension strategies taught for reading for meaning. There is a third dimension to listening, however, that is essential in effective teaching.

This third level of listening is the kind of careful listening we use as we observe the learners, notice their reactions, and watch their eyes to see if they 'get it.' We need to know if they are learning and what they are learning, and this takes close attentive listening.

This is the kind of listening that includes 'reading' the faces of the students as we teach. This is the kind of listening we use when assessing reading and the other language arts: we listen to them read, for example, determining by their tone and expression (among other things) whether they 'get it.'

Going back to an elementary classroom has made me newly aware of this kind of listening. I realize I am better at this with young learners, watching their fresh, eager faces: they openly display their joy and satisfaction when they get it, and they show their dismay and puzzlement when they don't get it. With adult learners, this is a work in progress for me. Their faces are not always as open; often, they are looking down into their laptops. This whole area, I now realize, is certainly worth further investigation.

Teacher as writer

Looking at myself as a writer chiefly involves my pursuits as a researcher. Because I have considered my research as fairly separate from the practicalities of teaching, I don't often share with the students in my course what I am writing about in my research. This may be partly a kind of modesty (*why would they be interested in my esoteric research?*). It may also stem from an awareness of the tensions between what is perceived as theoretical versus what is practical and the resistances to the more theoretical aspects of education (*aren't they here to learn how to become teachers?*). However, if I am to be honest and true to the principle about teaching from who I am, there is more that I could and should be sharing with preservice teachers about my research and writing. There are some research areas relevant to their becoming teachers of literacy.

I am interested in researching the changing definitions of literacy in the face of the new literacies. However, I am also motivated by my desire to return the definition of literacy to its oral roots, or at least, to maintain its grounding in those roots. This seems to increase in importance as life in the 21st century takes us deeper into technologically-driven communication and further away from face-to-face spoken communication. Maintaining a balance here can be a real challenge in a Bachelor of Education program that is officially designated as a 'laptop program.' On a daily basis, it becomes all too easy to slip from using a laptop as a tool for improving learning, particularly in the areas of reading and written communication, to one that becomes a distraction and an impediment to interpersonal listening and spoken communication. And yet, listening and speaking are crucial to teaching effectively. They closely connect to the teaching of reading and writing.

This has led me back into the elementary classroom to conduct my current research into the connections between storytelling (speaking and listening) and story writing. By 'getting up near the learners,' I am hoping to achieve further insight into the oral roots of literacy.

Final Comments

I have focused on myself as reader, speaker, listener and writer. I might also share who I am as a viewer (I belong to a film club, and I view and read about films as often as I can), and as a representer (I love theatre and visual arts, sometimes making amateur attempts in those areas). I may occasionally discuss a film informally with students, but I don't talk about these interests with them unless it is directly tied to instructional purposes. For example, as a writer, I write poetry for myself, but I share that only when modelling the teaching of poetry in the elementary classroom. I am a fairly private person, and I believe part of professionalism includes maintaining a healthy distance between personal and professional relationships.

Finally, as I teach the Language and Literacy course over time, I continue to grapple with how complex it all is, and how much material I want to cover. I am beginning to find a deeper appreciation for what really matters. What really matters is that I let the teacher candidates 'get up near the teacher' by teaching from who I am. What really matters is that I convey my passion for reading, writing, listening, and speaking. In terms of how to teach these language arts, I throw a lot of seeds in their direction. Often, they don't recognize them until they sprout later in the classroom, while on placement sometimes, or when teaching in their own classrooms. They send me emails declaring, "I didn't really understand it then, but now I see how it works" or they write, "it all makes sense now." Sometimes when they 'get up near the teacher' they don't get it right away. It is not always easy for me to stay patient about the time teaching and learning takes, but is always worth the wait.

Teachers teach that knowledge waits.
❦ Bob Dylan

The Importance of Confusion in Curriculum Development

Kurt Clausen

EVERY YEAR SINCE I BEGAN TEACHING Curriculum Development and Evaluation, I have engaged my students in a short exercise. At the beginning of the course, I ask them to fill out a Likert-scale questionnaire that situates their beliefs towards education, and works through their definition of 'curriculum' and how they would implement it. The same survey is given to them at the end of the year.

When I came up with this idea, I had the grand hypothesis that my students would come to the program as blank slates, with no strong ideas about anything technical, and would fill in most of their responses as neutral. I had great aspirations that throughout the year the staff, the teaching experience, and especially my course would go far in molding their minds, thereby giving them strong opinions about the definition of curriculum and how they would approach it.

To my baffled mind, the complete reverse occurred: most of the surveys were extremely strong at the beginning of the year (and generally polarized). At the end of the course, however, students waffled, had more neutral opinions, and gave support to many statements that were in contrast to one another. The more I looked at the results, the more puzzled and irritated I became. Had my teaching meant so little? Had I not tried to guide them to make choices and take firm stances?

I related this apparent discrepancy to a student and was thunderstruck by her response. Showing no surprise, she shrugged and said, "what d'ya expect?" I quizzed her further, and she gave me her sage reasoning. When students came here they were not children: most were in their early to mid-twenties, and some were considerably older. Throughout their academic careers, they had been told to have strong opinions and to defend their arguments. As my student informed me, most had no ego issues and were quite willing to make judgments, even when they had not gathered all the facts. Some had children, and all had been exposed to 'the curriculum' as students themselves. As such, most had experienced the school system enough to render a verdict on the term. Indeed, according to the initial findings, most thought of the curriculum as a prescription handed down from the Ministry to be inserted into the students' brains.

While this supposition began to sink in, my student then hit me with the uppercut point she was trying to make. Rather than just giving more information, this year of "teacher education" had, in actuality, confused students and shaken them to their core. Had I not repeatedly shown them that the curriculum could be defined in a number of different ways? Had I not shown them that, depending on their definition, they could go in many directions with course creation, implementation, and student assessment? Indeed, I try to base all sections of my course on the same root questions: "What do you believe students should learn, and how do you see them reaching that learning?" The answers each student teacher gives then determines how s/he views the process of education. In turn, this shapes how the student-teacher behaves as a course designer, educator and evaluator.

I first try to acquaint the students with some of the underlying, foundational beliefs that must be established before a course of study is even thought about. The forty students are separated into seven groups, and each given an -ism. In order, they are Zen Buddhism, Idealism, Humanism, Essentialism, Progressivism, Behavioralism and Reconstructionism. Of course, these are just a few general orientations (or philosophies) out of a myriad, but they do illustrate the point that many schools of conflicting ideas exist when developing curriculum. I assign each group a series of authors to read, and ask them to create a class based on the orientation. The students are to teach the class as an educator from this philosophy would teach, use the same class management techniques, rewards, punishments, evaluations, content, and so on.

Initially, most students seem quite happy at this apparently simple task: just follow along and apply a set dogma. Then they spot the readings I have assigned, and they tend to get quite intimidated. Rather than a 'how-to' manual of generic and restrained directions, the readings are quite bold, uninhibited, and individualistic. The ideas expressed by the authors were radical when they were written, and most are still radical today. In the group "Idealism", for example, I include excerpts from Plato, Robert Maynard Hutchins, and discussions of the Socratic Method; for "Humanism", Rousseau and A.S. Neill. Dewey's work forms the basis of "Progressivism", Skinner's of "Behavioralism", and Freire's of "Reconstructionism".

After finishing the readings, but before the 'mock class', each group meets with me to discuss what they have planned. Here is where I see the transformation in their attitude towards the curriculum: where this dry theory meets their pragmatic attitudes. One of my most entertaining and productive encounters occurred two years ago, when five very serious-looking students entered my office, sat down, and said nothing for a few moments.

Sensing something was bubbling under the surface, I decided to remain quiet as well, and waited for them to launch the first volley. Like dominos, each head turned to the one they had obviously nominated as the spokesperson. Her first words came out apologetic but forceful.

"Um, sir . . . you're having us do this Humanism orientation. But the readings you assigned were by these guys: Rousseau, Pestalozzi and A.S. Neill . . ." I nodded and smiled enigmatically.

"Uh," she continued. "But how can we do a good job when these guys are obviously nutjobs!?"

Suppressing a grin, I countered. "Okay, why are they crazy?"

"Well, you'd never get anything done in their classes."

"What would you never get done?"

"Real learning!" she concluded.

"And what is real learning?"

From there we had an extremely rich discussion on the fundamentals of what constituted an education, what should be taught, how it should be organized, how it should be evaluated. In the end, I realized that they had made the leap: rather than looking at curriculum as something to be followed, it was something to be discussed, debated, and decided upon in their own classroom. From this meeting came a very enlightening 'mock-class' that showed great student-centred principles of teaching few classmates had considered valid before.

Once the class has wrestled with the debate of 'canon versus dialog' when thinking about the curriculum, it then moves on to the more practical application of curriculum development. It is very tempting to make this a 'fill-in-the-blanks' exercise, as its whole purpose is to teach students how to create a practical, working unit plan that they may use out in practice teaching. A number of my student-teachers would, in all probability, be happier to see it done this way. However, I have found it of pivotal importance to tie it to the earlier "orientations" section. How you define the curriculum, and how you think a course should be taught, will inevitably dictate how you create a lesson plan, a unit plan, a yearly schedule, or indeed an entire educational system. And the teacher must know how to balance his/her beliefs with that of the job description.

When my student-teachers accept a position in the public school system, they have to understand that they are "buying into" certain values of that system. In Ontario, this presently means an increased governmental concern with accountability: with a desire to know how effective schools are in teaching students the fundamentals of reading, writing, adding, subtracting. It is important, therefore, that teachers create efficient mechanisms to help keep track of their students' educational progress, of what resources will be used, of what should be taught and what was previously learned. However, to stop here would be to countermand everything for which the teaching profession stands.

I choose the word *profession* carefully, and use it frequently in class. In its original sense it was "a declaration or vow made on entering . . . a religious order; vocation, calling, especially one that involves some branch of learning . . ." (*Concise Oxford Dictionary*, 1936, p. 919). To stay true to this profession, they must understand the latitude that they possess in choosing the various paths to set goals. In the particular classroom setting, they are the professionals; they cannot simply follow the government, their professors, the community, or the board. They have to act authentically according to their beliefs about what is right for the situation.

I ask my students "who were the worst and who were the best teachers in your memory?" Inevitably, they respond that the worst ones followed a pattern, read from the book, were boring. For these teachers, the plans had been laid out by the textbook. The best: the students always mention the exciting, the engaging, the active teachers; the ones who always seemed to act spontaneously and left the students marveling at what would come next. What separated these two teacher archetypes? "Planning" is my simple response. The first teacher left the planning up to others, followed the blueprint, and gave up his/her professional beliefs. The ones who had continually pulled "spontaneous" magic tricks out of thin air had, in all likelihood, put in threefold planning-time compared to the former. Planning not only allowed these teachers to meet the government-generated expectations, but enabled them to do it in a way that helped them stay true to their profession and orientation.

In the end, therefore, I have come to believe that my student was right: the object of the course I teach is not to inculcate the students into the "right" ways of the curriculum developer, teacher, or evaluator, but to spin them around and shake up their preconceptions of the role. In Medieval times, people became so identified with their craft that they frequently took on its names as their own: someone who made barrels became known as "Cooper"; a person who created arrows was called "Fletcher". Each did the same job that his father had trained him to do without variation. What I hope to accomplish in this program is to husband graduates into the teaching profession who will not use the epithet "teacher" to limit themselves: filled with dogma of past generations to mindlessly carry out the same task. Rather, I hope to start students on their teaching careers from a point of confusion.

Again, I turn to the dictionary to show *confusion*'s true meaning of "throw into disorder; mix up the mind" (*Concise Oxford Dictionary*, 1936, p. 237). The last thing new teachers should possess is a fixed order in their mind, especially if it is one put there by a professor who thinks he knows how a class should work. It is much more important for new teachers to leave university with a nascent ability to use their future experiences to continually question their actions (whether it be creating unit plans, evaluating students, grading or evaluating the curriculum themselves) and what they see around them.

A Paradigm Shift

Julie Corkett

When I was told that I would be teaching Educational Psychology and Special Education, it completed the circle of my education experiences. I had been a product of special education programs, and now I would be the teacher. During the development of the course, I spent a great deal of time reflecting on my experiences as a special education student, as a classroom teacher, and as a researcher. It was from these experiences that I formulated the lessons that I wanted to share with preservice teachers.

As a special education student, I had learned from my teachers that I was a hopeless cause; that a student who had reading difficulties could never be expected to amount to much. I learned that I did not have to take math in high school because I was too stupid. I learned that I should be thankful for graduating from high school. I learned that special education students were different from other students in our abilities to reason, to participate, and to function in a classroom environment. During my first week as a university student, I was told that I would never amount to much because I could not spell. I learned then that maybe my teachers were wrong. I had made it to university, just like the normal kids, so maybe I wasn't so different after all. This is the first lesson that I give preservice teachers. I want them to understand how quickly students' learning experiences can be turned into feelings of inadequacy that may stay with them throughout their lives. I want them to realize that it is not the weaknesses, but the strengths that define students' abilities.

Many of the students in the Bachelor of Education program have not truly experienced what it is like grapple with learning. They have not had the opportunity to experience what it is like to struggle with a concept that others grasp with ease, or to combat feelings of inadequacy daily. Since preservice teachers may lack this experience, it may be difficult for them to appreciate the daily educational experiences of students with exceptionalities. To provide the teacher candidates with the brief and superficial opportunity to experience the learning process from the perspective of students with exceptionalities and/or learning difficulties, the teacher candidates are provided with the opportunity to learn a new skill with which they have had no prior experience (e.g., knitting or tying knots). For the students who took this activity seriously, they began to appreciate what it must be like to struggle with a skill or to have someone repeat instructions over and over and over again. They expressed surprise at how quickly feelings of inadequacy occurred, and how they fought the overwhelming the desire to give up. They realized that if rational adults who do not have an exceptionality must combat these feelings, how much more overwhelming these feelings must be for children with exceptionalities and learning difficulties. By the end of the activity, the preservice teachers understood the impact emotions and feelings have on the learning process, and how quickly they began to define themselves based on what they could not do instead of what they could do.

As a teacher, I learned that there were teachers who continued to see students with exceptionalities and/or learning difficulties as not belonging in the *regular* classroom. I learned that were teachers who viewed a diversified classroom as a detriment rather than as a unique opportunity. I learned that some teachers believe that since students with exceptionalities and/or learning difficulties may have trouble with tasks involving higher-level thinking, they should be exempt from such tasks. I want the preservice teachers to leave behind the belief that there is an entirely different set of learning theories and classroom and behavior management strategies that are applicable to individuals with exceptionalities and learning difficulties. I want them to understand that there isn't a secret formula for teaching students with exceptionalities. I want them to learn that while individuals with exceptionalities have different learning abilities and strategies than children without learning difficulties, they still have value; and if taught the proper learning strategies, they are capable of exceeding the boundaries of their difficulties. I want them to understand that students' self-esteem, self-concept, and self-efficacy can all be destroyed when teachers focus on what students cannot do instead of what they can do. The Inuit call teachers *people makers*, but teachers must also understand that they can be *people destroyers*: destroying dreams, hopes, and selves, leaving a sense of helplessness and indifference in their wake.

To assist the preservice teachers in appreciating the potential impact of teachers on a child's education, they are provided with the opportunity to examine Individual Education Plans from the perspective of the classroom teacher, the resource teacher, the teacher's aid, and the parent. This exercise enables preservice teachers to discover inconsistencies between the teacher's perspective of a student's abilities and the parent's perspectives, with one party either setting expectations too high or too low. Others found that teachers focused on what the child could not do and not on their strengths. Still others found teachers struggling with the desire to do more for their students, but were unable to because of classroom size and/or because of lack of funding. The teacher candidates began to realize that special education is not simply learning a secret formula designed to *fix* students, but that it is a complex issue involving parents, politics, and personal biases: all of which impact the student.

As a researcher, I have learned that it is not abnormal nor the exception to the rule for a student with exceptionalities and/or learning difficulties to obtain academic and career success. I want preservice teachers to know and accept this truth. By sharing my personal experiences and knowledge, I want the teacher candidates to view students with learning difficulties and exceptionalities as individuals who are capable of meeting their dreams when they are provided with a teacher who enables the students to believe in themselves. Once that belief in oneself has been removed or destroyed, it can take a lifetime to rebuild. To meet this goal, I introduced preservice teachers to the application of metacognition and strategic learning. With an understanding of these two processes, the preconceived notion that students with exceptionalities and/or learning difficulties are unable to work and learn at the higher levels of thinking may be destroyed.

Thus, rather than denying students with exceptionalities and/or learning difficulties the opportunity to process information at a higher level, it is important to provide them with the strategies that they need. For these students, it is often the strategies that are lacking, not the ability.

By the end of the course, the majority of preservice teachers leave with a feeling of contentment. For some, this feeling of contentment comes from developing an understanding of their own learning difficulties, and by noticing that their fellow classmates no longer view their exceptionality with scorn. Others feel contentment because they are no longer afraid of the term “special education”. They appreciate that special education is not about working with exceptionalities and learning difficulties, but it is about working with individuals. Special education is the embracing and application of diversification.

Unfortunately, it is discouraging to know that each year there will be one or two preservice teachers who will still not fully embrace the issues surrounding special education. These preservice teachers are able to give the politically correct argument for inclusion, while personally maintaining the belief that inclusion is fine as long as it does not occur in their classroom. They also continue to hold the belief that having a classroom with students with exceptionalities and/or Individual Education Plans is not the norm.

Finally, there will still be others who continue to seek that “secret formula” that can be used to *fix* students with exceptionalities and/or learning difficulties. For this handful of students, their understanding and appreciation for special education will not truly begin until they have a classroom of their own.

Teaching Curriculum Methods:

Instructional Techniques

Ray Davis

THROUGHOUT MY PRESERVICE TEACHING EXPERIENCE, the phrase "the tip of the iceberg" is often heard during the 'Methods' classes that I have the pleasure of instructing. In my opinion, this may well describe both the joy and the frustration that is often encountered in this area of the Bachelor of Education program.

As my course outline illustrates, Methods involves introducing students to a wide variety of pedagogical concepts. Included in this list are the political realm (curriculum, government policy, assessment, professional standards), planning (yearly, unit, and lesson), current initiatives (multiple intelligences, Action Research, technology), and teaching strategies (cooperative learning, differentiating instruction, learning centres, technology, assessment techniques). Somewhere within our limited timeline, students must learn to communicate effectively, to plan using several formats, be able to assess all of the various intelligences authentically, and to be reflective practitioners.

Although the wealth of topics create a stimulating program, they also lead to the phenomenon described earlier, the "tip of the iceberg" approach, whereby I am able to merely tease them by introducing them to many exciting ideas while being unable to investigate any of them fully.

As with any course or workshop that I have been involved in, my personal priorities have always been to introduce students or practicing teachers to as many teaching strategies as possible, and provide resources with which they can begin their personal journeys. In Methods, these goals have always been tempered by the necessity to introduce specific content. In my case, this involves such topics as the dynamics of the Ontario curriculum, the Standards of Practice for the Teaching Profession expected by Ontario's College of Teachers, the teaching resources available within the Ontario Curriculum Unit Planner, the different versions of the Ontario Report Card, and the unique planning formats advocated within our teacher education program.

In any course, the personality of the instructor or professor soon becomes transparent to students. They quickly recognize the essence of the individual: the few qualities that each of us believe are critical to our success in the classroom. Our personal "quirks" are frequently discussed over coffee, or good-naturedly mimicked during the various presentations at the holiday concert in December. In my case, I would hope that this would involve my passionate belief that teaching is about "relationships", and that everything we do in the classroom relates to that belief. Additionally, I would hope that there are few students who can spend that many hours in my tutelage without realizing the importance of allowing students to assume considerable responsibility for the learning process in everything from collaboratively establishing the rules and routines to the planning, implementation, and assessment of program. A constant reminder is offered that everything we do in the classroom is done for one purpose: the effective education of our students. We always attempt to challenge each student to be the best s/he can be and attempt to offer them a supportive climate in which to make that possible.

Further to this, the popularity of Jeanne Gibbs' "Tribes" program in the province of Ontario has proven to be beneficial in this regard.

One of my favorite quotes is that "they may not always remember what you taught them, but they will always remember how you treated them". Another frequent reminder is about the influence we have as teachers on the children we teach.

On a personal level, my program strongly advocates a number of specific beliefs. The first lies in the area of learning styles and multiple intelligences. Having had the opportunity to listen to Howard Gardner and study many of his writings, this has become one of my major foci. On many occasions, I can be heard to muse that this would be one of the areas that I personally would attempt to investigate, and around which my classroom would be organized. We often discuss the importance of beginning our teaching year by endeavoring to determine the personal learning styles or intelligences within our new group of learners. For this reason, we complete inventories to identify our own dominant intelligences or learning preferences and illustrate that we can be "smart" in different ways.

A second belief involves the importance of our teaching environment. Within this topic, I include not only the organization of our classroom time, space, and resources, but also the establishment of a positive classroom climate in which all students can achieve their best results. This was frequently an interview question that I asked during my years as an educational administrator in the elementary panel. In asking this question, it is my belief that I am able to determine a prospective teacher's personal teaching style as well as his/her philosophy of classroom management: always of interest to administrators. In the consecutive program, we are involved minimally with classroom management, since it is taught in a separate course. However, in my concurrent classes, I frequently investigate many concepts related to managing a classroom: a topic that is always well received since it is a huge concern for a beginning teacher.

Finally, a focus within my personal approach to Methods involves teaching strategies. During my years in the classroom, my belief was that students learned more effectively within a collaborative environment. To that goal, an emphasis in my course often involves collaborative and cooperative learning. An attempt is made not only to introduce the education students to these teaching and organizational strategies, but also to provide them with resources to enable them to experiment with some ideas during their latter practice teaching assignments. Several strategies are modeled in class, including the creation of paper airplanes and the use of a variety of Spencer Kagan's cooperative learning structures to introduce much of the content that I have noted earlier: an example being the use of the Jigsaw structure in familiarizing students with the expectations of the College of Teachers in the Standards of Practice document, or the use of a Placemat to investigate the documents on differentiating instruction. This definitely falls under the topic of "walking the talk", since the use of examples of the topics you discuss is so vital to the comprehension of the topic. Describing a cooperative structure is much easier when it is used to demonstrate a theme. Beginning classes with a Rally table or Round Robin illustrates the point you endeavor to make. Organizing them into groups for a Jigsaw Expert allows them to explore considerably more content than I could ever hope to accomplish.

Teaching adult learners is a fascinating experience. They bring their wealth of personal backgrounds to your class. Some have been incredibly positive, and have aided their decision to become teachers. Others may have been less positive, but those experiences have also helped to create a desire to teach for quite a different reason. In addition, our students often bring a wide range of work experiences with many having been in the private sector as social workers, financial advisors, parents, or other previous occupations. Sharing these many perspectives can be an incredibly enriching experience. Watching them develop a teaching philosophy and both assimilate and reject the many ideas to which they are introduced is an honor. Trying to provide them with a solid base of "instructional strategies" in Curriculum Methods is an amazing voyage. It is one that I am delighted to have been able to share.

"What's It All About, Alfie?"

Developing a Personal Philosophy of Teaching

Todd A. Horton

I THINK EVERYONE SHOULD STOP and reflect on their teaching from time to time. It is only by thinking about what we do, how we do it, and – most importantly – *why* we're doing it that we gain balance, and a much-needed sense of purpose. I see this as somewhat analogous to stopping and looking at an aesthetically pleasing view: a sunset, possibly a favourite piece of ocean, or even an awe-inspiring cityscape. It is by stopping and 'soaking up the view' that one gains perspective on life, and begins to find an answer to the question asked by Bill Naughton in his 1963 play: "What's it all about, Alfie?"

As I consider what I believe is most important to impart to teacher candidates in my current position at a Canadian faculty of education, I have, after much consideration, settled on two points.

First, recognize that you will have moments of doubt as to what you're doing. This is not a bad thing, indeed, it is probably imperative. Embrace these moments of doubt as an opportunity to question what you are doing and why you're doing it. Only then can you begin to answer the question posed above.

Second, as you begin to answer said question, begin formulating it into a personal philosophy of teaching. It doesn't have to be particularly grand, to be sure it is probably best to keep it simple and adaptable, so it can grow with you as you mature in your understanding of teaching and learning.

With this in mind, I usually convey these points in the form of an autobiographical story that goes something like this . . .

I vividly recall my first year of teaching. It was hell, no other word for it. It wasn't that the students were particularly difficult – they weren't – but I was having a difficult time grappling with what I was doing in the classroom. Not in the sense that I didn't know what to teach or even how to teach it (the curriculum documents helped me with that). No, my problem was I didn't know why I was teaching at all!

Quite frankly, the daily grind of teaching had caused me to lose my sense of purpose. I felt like I was on a treadmill that rolled round and round, day after day, with no end in sight, save a holiday weekend or end of school year. I seemed to forget all my learning from the Bachelor of Education program, and was resorting to cheap theatrics and quick fixes. By the third month, I had tapped out my bag of tricks – you know, the fun activities that keep students quiet for a while because they are mildly entertaining, but really have dubious educational value – and I was struggling to survive. I would wake up anxious each morning, wondering if I could tread water another day and knowing full well that drowning was increasingly becoming inevitable. I began to resent the students, the school, and myself. Thoughts of "getting out" started to creep into my head as I asked myself, "am I cut out for this?"

It is at times like this that serendipity can occur, and it certainly did for me. I found myself attending some sort of function one evening, after a particularly difficult day at school. Was it an academic, charity, or social event? I can't recall exactly, but I know it was being held at the local university.

Among the guests was a professor whom I'd been a student of a few years earlier. I remembered him as a stellar professor, a model teacher whom everyone wanted to emulate in the classroom.

He shook my hand, and cordially inquired how and what I was doing; strangely, I found myself telling him everything! Words tumbled out of my mouth as I confessed my struggles in the classroom, how I couldn't seem to engage the students, and how I was thinking of "retiring" from teaching.

For a moment, he stood motionless and blank-faced, probably considering how to escape the man having a breakdown in front of him. Then he began to speak to me in a way that would ultimately change my approach to teaching, and – in some sense – change my life as a whole.

"Todd, why did you become a teacher in the first place?" Though the question was asked gently, I wanted to shrink back in embarrassment; I felt that even he was questioning whether I should be in the classroom. "Don't misunderstand me. I'm not questioning your fitness, I remember you to be very capable. I'm talking about what drew you to teaching as a profession, as a service to society."

I hesitated momentarily, perhaps considering if I truly had the strength to engage in a philosophical discussion that could psychologically unnerve me.

"I don't know . . . I suppose it was to be a service to society, as you say. I wanted to offer my skills to help others become who they can be. I guess it sounds trite, but I wanted to help young people see the world in a more dynamic, varied way than perhaps I did at their age."

My former professor listened attentively before interjecting, "it sounds to me like you might be worrying more about teaching the curriculum than teaching the students: the very people you wanted to help in the beginning".

I had to admit he might be right. In the last little while, students' faces were becoming a blur. They were "the class" in my mind, a group, a mass of emotionally needy people, rather than separate individuals on their own life journeys. Still . . . how does one deal with each student as an individual, while addressing the curriculum that I'm accountable for?

He continued, "Let me ask you this: what exactly are you hoping for these young people?"

"Hoping for?" I asked, confused. "I don't follow."

The professor leaned closer, and said in a low voice, "Teaching is not about the curriculum, it's about students. You have to decide what you hope for these young people, what you want for them as they grow up, leave school, and become people with whom we share society. Aren't you preparing them to live in the world with us? Once you know what kind of person you hope for, then you tailor the curriculum and your teaching style to make that happen for each of the students in your class . . . while respecting their individuality."

I leaned back and looked at him as if he were speaking in tongues. Didn't he realize that I was at the point where keeping students from killing each other, and perhaps me, was all I hoped for!

My former professor smiled. "I don't have all the answers, my boy, and I certainly can't answer the question of what you hope for when teaching your students, only you can do that, but I can suggest this. Try writing down all the things you believe young people need to know and do, as well as the values you hope they'll embrace, then formulate it into a paragraph or two – almost like a personal philosophy of teaching. Once completed, you'll have a touchstone or reference that will guide you in making choices about what and how to teach. You'll have purpose, and nothing says you can't return to it from time to time to reorient yourself when things feel like they're going awry. I do it all the time."

Many years have passed since that fateful night, and even though I left with more questions than answers, I've come to understand what my professor was talking about. It's about citizenship, and having a vision of what type of citizen you wish to foster through your teaching, and then making choices that help you achieve your goal. It's kind of like design-down unit and lesson planning. You have to have an idea of where you want to end up, so you can plan how to get there. Now, like lesson plans, one has to respect the individual nature of the students. My vision – my personal teaching philosophy if you will – has to be broad enough and flexible enough to accommodate individual student's needs and aspirations. Nevertheless, I think a "road map" of sorts is incredibly helpful for maintaining focus, particularly when the daily grind of teaching can easily distract from the larger sense of purpose.

As students listen to this story, I usually see heads nodding in understanding, along with a healthy peppering of furrowed brows and other quizzical looks as some struggle to grasp the story's meaning. I like telling this story, but it – among other things – tempers students' desire to obtain a list of "fun" activities with the belief that that is what teaching is about. Further, I use this story to offset any desire students may have to assume my philosophical approach to teaching as if it is a blueprint that can be transferred from professor to student, from person to person. I always end the narrative by emphasizing that it was I who had to develop my own personal philosophy of teaching: no one else could do it for me, because no one else is quite like me, and no one else would have to implement it in a classroom with students quite like mine. I also underscore the point that I've composed many personal philosophies of teaching over the years, revising them as I grew as a teacher. Students need to realize that this is a living document, always provisional, never complete.

Of course, I ask students to begin the task of composing their own personal philosophy of teaching. Some relish the prospect, others resist. Some of the enthused quickly become frustrated, others struggle in the beginning only to have "light bulb" moments whereby it all begins to make sense. Such is the incredible diversity of people in the world. To assist in this venture, students are assigned a number of readings on citizenship education. Many educators, particularly in the field of social studies, have developed concepts that serve as helpful thinking tools for designing personal "road maps" for teaching.

Does this help a young teacher candidate answer the question "what's it all about, Alfie?" Maybe, maybe not, but I'd like to think so. After all, it's now seventeen years from that fateful meeting with my former professor, and I'm still going strong and loving every minute of my life in the classroom.

First & Lasting Impressions:

Teaching Future Science Teachers How to Teach Science

Gerald Laronde

SCIENCE IS RICH and endlessly fascinating, filled with wonder; it arouses curiosity and creates an appreciation of our progress throughout history, as well as a greater awareness of our natural surroundings in the world and universe. Teaching Science teachers 'how to teach' involves modeling the skills to become an effective practitioner, problem solver, and critical thinker. A teacher of Science enlightens students about their moral and ethical responsibilities to society, the environment, and their future students.

My area of pedagogy involves guiding and facilitating the development of Science teachers in a Bachelor of Education (B. Ed.) program; essentially, I will briefly focus on 'how to teach Science' linking examples of methodology and curriculum studies of a first lesson to theory and practice.

Miller and Seller (1990) state that "curriculum is an explicitly and implicitly intentional set of interactions designed to facilitate learning and development and to impose meaning on experience" (p.3). Curriculum Studies is a broad term; therefore, I will focus on some selected teaching/learning strategies that B. Ed. students would experience in my classroom.

In order to be effectively taught, Science, as well as many other disciplines, should incorporate as many curriculum methodologies as possible. A teacher should have a repertoire of teaching methods available that can be used at anytime. Different content areas or skills may be taught more effectively using a particular teaching method. What follows is a description of how I typically start my Senior Science elective course, incorporating a critical teaching method, modeling.

I raise my hand and wait until I have everyone's attention, and then state: "Grade 9, I will be demonstrating several different scenarios up here, and I want you to observe them all quietly. Try to think about what they all have in common, and how they may be linked." I then perform four little skits that introduce the topics that will be taught in the course over the year.

I don a farmer's hat, and have a straw hanging out of my mouth. I pantomime a short skit in which a farmer plants two seeds of corn. He cares for each plant, watching them grow. He fertilizes one plant by placing the anther to the tassel, and the other he chooses not to. To the farmer's surprise, the end result is that the fertilized plant has a cob of corn with kernels, and the other has none.

Without a word, I doff the farmer's hat, put the corn away, and put on a lab coat. I continue on, drawing a model of the atom on the board. I turn to the class, scratching my head with a puzzled look. Slowly an "Ah ah!" look of understanding comes over my face, and I smile mischievously at the class.

Next, I pretend to take a telescope and peer into the heavens. I pull out a guitar and sing, Eric Idle's "The Galaxy Song", which appeared in a Monty Python skit a while back. The second time, I encourage the whole class to sing along with me to the words on an overhead, and they always do.

Finally, I dim the lights and pull out a fluorescent light tube. I ask for a 'victim' or volunteer to come up and place the tube near a static electrical source like a Van de Graaf generator. I warn the student about the hazards of getting injured if they touch the metal ends. I stress the importance of being safe, and talk of how I don't want to lose a student right away. The fluorescent tube lights up in their hand.

I ask the class while raising my hand, "Alright grade nine, quietly raise your hand if you think you know the connection between these four little skits or demonstrations." I wait for a few hands to rise, and I call on students to give their hypothesis. I accept a few answers, thanking the students for their responses and for raising their hand.

Invariably, sometimes with prompting, I do get the answer that I am looking for. The four skits represent the four topics that will be taught throughout the grade nine Science course. The strands and topics are: 1) Biology: Reproduction, 2) Chemistry: Atoms and Elements 3) Earth and Space Science: The Study of the Universe, and 4) Physics: The Characteristics of Electricity. I would then review the skits, linking each one to the strands and title of that topic from the Ontario Curriculum Science Grades 9-10 (p.9) on the overhead.

Coming out of the role playing, I welcome the students back to the faculty of education Science class, and ask the B. Ed. students what I was hoping to accomplish as a teacher with this introduction to a grade nine class.

The list of responses usually include: to create an interest in Science and the course, to integrate other areas of the curriculum in the teaching of Science such as drama and music, to create a physically safe environment for the learners with respect to the electricity and their ability to participate actively in the class, to get the students to think critically and hypothesize, to use role playing as a teaching tool, and to explore the use of humor as a motivational technique in a lesson.

There is one response that is rarely mentioned, and sometimes requires prompting. I ask the students to think, because they are missing a very important purpose that they as new teachers must consider. I have established class control using a management tool, which is raising a hand and waiting to be called upon prior to speaking.

With a strong introduction, I have motivated and engaged the learners, 'hooking' their attention. I have established my presence as a teacher immediately, and a classroom rule subtly and effectively, while creating an interest in Science and teaching content. I emphasize the importance of classroom management in all teaching, especially Science for safety reasons.

I then take time to play a 'name game' to get to know all of the students' names. After this, I hand out and discuss the course outline.

There are several models of teaching integrated into this first lesson, which are described by key theorists in the literature. The concept of presenting the students with a cognitive framework structure, such as the four topics to be taught during the semester, is an example of an advance organizer model suggested by David Ausubel (Friend, Bursuck & Hutchison, 1998, p. 279). He believes that the presentation and organization of information is important, and often enhance student understanding of ideas and their relationships (Joyce & Weil, 1996, p. 267).

The scenario presented is reflective of a role playing situation. Role playing is a method I use throughout the year. I often have students role play that they are in a class at a certain grade, to the point that I actually plant typical behavior problems in the class. A real class does, in fact, have these management issues and it is unrealistic to teach in an environment where these behaviors do not exist. Role playing is classified by Joyce and Weil (1996, p. 14) as a model of teaching falling within the social family; it is effective in discussing social issues, developing social skills and social behavior.

The lesson itself and the follow up questions are examples of direct instruction, which is often an effective model of teaching (Joyce & Weil, 1996, p. 343).

The lecture method falls into direct instruction, and for some students is an efficient and reliable method of delivering key information. However, to make a lecture successful, the content should be presented with enthusiasm and some humor. Narratives with personal meaning that connect the learners with the content greatly enhance a lecture. Engaging the learners with thought provoking questions often keeps them on task. Pre-assessing strengths and needs of the learners prior to the lesson and observing their behavior as the lesson progresses will help gauge the proper length of time for that style of delivery, and if any modifications to the strategy are required. Hergenhan and Olsen (1993) state that there are at least three conditions where the use of the lecture is justified. One is where the material or content is new; another where the lecturer is a prominent individual; and third, in which the lecturer can create interest with enthusiasm, and with the method of presentation.

Science is not a stand alone subject. Teaching can be enhanced by integrating other subject areas into Science, such as Music, Art, Drama, Mathematics, Physical Education, Geography, History, and certainly Language Arts. All other subjects can be successfully integrated into Science by various means. The teacher must plan well, and be creative when incorporating other subject areas into Science, or vice versa. The introduction to the lesson described in the opening scenario included both drama and music.

This introductory lesson addresses some of the Multiple Intelligences described by Gardner (1993), specifically musical intelligence with the song and interpersonal intelligence with the drama. Ideally, a teacher would attempt to address all of the multiple intelligences throughout the course. This will require some extra planning on the teacher's part, but it will enable learners to enjoy learning about science from their strength.

The wide use of different teaching methods addresses several learning styles (Kolb, 1984). For experiential learning, it describes how the visual learner can see the various demonstrations at the front, how the auditory learner can hear through the use of music, and how the tactile-kinesthetic learner would be the volunteer who comes up to be the volunteer in the electricity demonstration. Science is a subject that can be easily taught using 'hands-on' learning, such as labs and activities that would appeal to the tactile learner. Students learn through their own experiences in and out of the classroom. Throughout the course, various activities in many lessons could be planned to incorporate learning styles of all the learners.

Memorization, as a model of teaching (Joyce & Weil, 1996, p. 209-231) is frequently used in Science. I start the year stating the importance of knowing all students' names as quickly as possible, and by playing a name game. In a class of about thirty to forty students, each person states the name of all of the people before them three times, so the last person (myself) will state the names of all the students. This ten to fifteen minute exercise is valuable in getting to know the group, and acts as an icebreaker, encouraging students to take a small risk, thus creating a sense of comfort, and preparing them to take greater risks in the future. In the teaching of content, mnemonic devices are valuable learning tools when students are required to remember large amounts of content. Students can create mnemonic devices for remembering the order of the planets, the periodic table, or the pathway of blood through the heart.

"All teachers worthy of the name are storytellers. It is through stories that we are best able to share with learners the vitality and relevance of our knowledge" (Wanner, 1994, p. 1). The narrative is one of the most powerful teaching tools. The history of telling stories exceeds the infancy of academic writing, and to this day captures the attention of the learner. The story ties content to meaning, links abstract to vicarious experience, and links cognitive to affective. Egan (1986) describes a model of how to use the power of the story form to teach any content, making it more meaningful and engaging (p.2).

> *Narrative . . . can also be a useful tool for analysis and for assimilating one's understanding of scientific and technical concepts (Booth & Barton, 2000, p. 9).*

The following is a story of how a student teacher used the narrative in teaching a lesson.

On the board, she neatly wrote down the agenda for the lesson. This was her final task in preparation for the lesson. She turned, smiled, and greeted the students as they entered the classroom and sat at their desks. On the other side of the board was the title "Ecology" and "The Mystery of the Reindeer on St. Matthew's Island".

Once they were settled, she asked the class, "Have you heard of the Mystery of the Reindeer on St. Matthew's Island?"

No hands went up.

She waited for a while for a response, and stated, "Then let me tell you."

Knowing she had captivated their attention, she said, "But first, you will have to solve the mystery just as the scientists did many years ago. I will read a bit of the story, and then you will have a chance to think like the scientists. First, I will let you listen to some of the facts and background of the story, and then you can form your own hypothesis on what you think happened to the reindeer."

She read some of the facts of the story, and then had the students write down their own hypothesis. They then shared their hypothesis with a partner, and then with the group of six that were sitting in their group, listing as many possible reasons as they could concerning what had happened to the animals. Slowly, she disseminated a few more of the observations that the scientists had discovered in regards to the massive die off of about 6000 reindeer. The students, after each bit of information, such as weather conditions, parasites, and predators, would then discuss this new information, and how it would influence their hypothesis. Eventually, after the final bit of information was given, a final hypothesis would be given from each group. This answer would compare with the hypothesis that the scientists developed.

The students would answer questions such as: factors affecting the fluctuation of population changes, the role that society played in introducing the population of reindeer on to the island, and the role of each organism within an ecosystem.

This teacher taught this lesson to her peers within the Bachelor of Education program at Nipissing University. She then evaluated herself, received feedback from her peers on her teaching, and an evaluation from the professor.

The student teacher effectively integrated the narrative with the scientific method. In 1965, Joseph Schwab worked on the Biological Sciences Curriculum Study (BSCS). This was designed to teach students skills similar to the methods of scientific investigation and inquiry used by biologists in the laboratory. Teaching with the BSCS model, one would start out with the premise that Science has a tentative nature. Scientists do not know everything, and must figure things out. Theories also change with new information. Second, the narrative of inquiry describes the history of major ideas in biology or the Sciences. Third, the laboratory is used to have students think and investigate problems (Joyce & Weil, 1996, p. 180-183).

There is some discussion regarding the definition of constructivism, but Reagan, Case, and Brubacher (2000) tend to define it as more of an epistemology. Constructivism is practiced within the B. Ed. Science classroom when students teach a lesson to their peers. Teaching this lesson provides the student with an opportunity for a practical and interactive learning experience. Students receive feedback from their peers and the professor in addition to their own reflection. Over the course of the program, they have practice teaching for thirteen weeks, during which they would be constructing knowledge from their knowledge of the curriculum and their interaction with students, faculty, and associate teachers.

Weeks (1997) notes that, as a teaching model, constructivists believe that learners build their own meaning using their existing conceptual frameworks, and their interpretation of incoming information. The B. Ed. students build knowledge on their teaching experiences. The variety of teaching methods that they see and experience contributes to their repertoire of teaching skills.

In 1897, John Dewey stated:

> *One of the greatest difficulties in the present teaching of Science is that the material is presented in purely objective form, or is treated as a new peculiar kind of experience which the child can add to that which he has already had. In reality, Science is of value because it gives the ability to interpret and control the experience already had. It should be introduced, not as so much new subject-matter, but as showing the factors already involved in previous experience and as furnishing tools by which that experience can be more easily and effectively regulated (Miller and Seller, 1990, p. 73).*

Student teachers are all required to teach a Science lesson from a topic in the curriculum from grades 7 to 10. This ensures that the students have familiarity with the curriculum. The lesson can be taught using a variety of suggested teaching models, but should include some 'hands-on' activity.

Other types of teaching methods used within the class include mastery learning, (Bigge & Shermis, 1999, p. 261) programmed instruction or programmed learning, computer assisted instruction, synectics, case studies, discrepant events, Science Inquiry, (Joyce & Weil, 1996) laboratories, hands-on activities, cooperative learning,

(Slavin, 1995) field trips, problem solving, Science fairs, and Science Olympics (Weeks, 1995). Each of these teaching models or strategies is taught and experienced by the student teachers. If constructivism is knowledge building on experiences, then the students build their bag of teaching tools through these learning experiences.

Miller and Seller (1990, p. 196) indicate criteria for selecting teaching models; initially, they suggest that chosen models should be congruent with one's aims and developmental goals. In summary, they state it is easier for a teacher to teach within a specific metaorientation if their philosophy is congruent with their familiar teaching models.

This does not mean that a teacher should only teach within their comfort zone of teaching. A teacher should be able to learn, adapt, experiment and flourish with other types of teaching models. All of these teaching models would become part of their teaching repertoire. A teacher can examine curriculum expectations, pre-assess the learners and the learning environment, and decide on the best teaching model for this part of the curriculum at this particular time.

Teaching someone how to teach Science is a complex task. It has many layers of theory as well as attitudes, skills and values. It can be considered an art to someone who finds it easy to do and yet a Science to someone who works hard at learning content and perfecting their craft.

When student teachers leave my class, they have the necessary teaching tools to be effective Science teachers. They have knowledge of a variety of teaching strategies, and the ability to choose the method best suited to teach individual concepts and skills.

Teachers should have a thirst for Science knowledge, and the passion to share that knowledge in order to tempt their future students and keep them yearning for more, not just through their course, but throughout their lives. Their passion and enthusiasm for teaching should ignite the minds and hearts of their students to establish a lifelong love of learning.

References

Bigge, M. L. & Shermis, S.S. (1999). *Learning theories for teachers* (6th ed.). Don Mills, ON: Addison Wesley Longman.

Booth, D. & Barton, B. (2000). *Storyworks: How teachers can use shared stories in the new curriculum*. Markham, ON: Pembroke Publishers.

Egan, K. (1986). *Teaching as story telling: An alternative approach to teaching and curriculum in the elementary school*. London, ON: The Althouse Press.

Friend, M., Bursack, W. & Hutchison, N. (1998). *Including Exceptional Students: A practical guide for classroom teachers*. Scarborough, ON: Prentice-Hall.

Gardner, H. (1993). *Multiple intelligences: The theory in practice*. NY: Basic Books

Henderson, J. G. (1996). *Reflective teaching: The study of your constructivist practices* (2nd ed.). Englewood Cliffs, NJ: Prentice-Hall.

Hergenhahn, B.R., & Olsen, M. H. (1992). *An introduction to the theories of learning*. 4th ed. Toronto: Prentice-Hall.

Joyce, B. R. & Weil, M. (1996). *Models of teaching*. Needham Heights, MA.: Allyn and Bacon.

Kolb, D. A. (1984) *Experiential Learning*, Englewood Cliffs, NJ.: Prentice Hall

Miller, J. P., & Seller, W. (1990). *Curriculum perspectives and practice*. Toronto, ON: Copp Clark Pitman.

Posner, G. J., (1995). *Analyzing the curriculum* (2nd ed.). Toronto: McGraw-Hill.

Reagan, T. G., Case, C. W. and Brubacher, J. W. (2000). *Becoming a reflective educator: How to build a culture of inquiry in the schools* (2nd ed.). Thousand Oaks, CA: Corwin Press.

Slavin, R. E., (1995). *Cooperative learning* (2nd ed.). Needham Heights, MA: Allyn and Bacon.

Ontario Ministry of Education and Training . (1999). *The Ontario Curriculum Grades 9 and 10: Science*. Toronto, ON: Queen's Printer for Ontario.

Wanner, S. Y. (1994). *On with the story: Adolescents learning through narrative*. Portsmouth, NH: Boyton/Cook.

Weeks, R. C. (1997). *The child's world of science and technology: A book for teachers*. Scarborough, ON: Prentice Hall, Allyn and Bacon.

I Too Was On a Journey

John S. Long

The Education and Schooling course deals with the historical, philosophical, legal, and social contexts of education in Ontario. Bachelor of Education (B.Ed.) candidates consider some of the educational philosophies in practice today, critically reflect on an incident or issue in the practicum, demonstrate an understanding of a personally-developed philosophy of teaching and learning, gain an understanding of the classroom as a social structure, and the role of the teacher as facilitator of social interaction and social development, and examine some of the laws that impact upon the classroom teacher.

Since we are a "laptop program," my course is accessible online. I provide a free collection of readings, assembled with the informed consent from the reflections of past B.Ed. candidates (Long "Welcome to Educ 4102"). Instead of requiring that candidates purchase an education law text, we access the Ontario Education Statutes and Regulations online; links are provided with Nipissing University's software image (Ontario; Canada; Ontario College of Teachers).

During their eight months of classes and placements, B. Ed. candidates are faced with numerous challenges, as well as successes. I remind primary/junior candidates that they are on "the B. Ed. journey." Since each of us is unique, I tell them to expect their experiences in the B. Ed. program to also be unique. Some compare the B. Ed. year to a diamond, for it is multifaceted. Some describe it as a zipped file, absolutely jam-packed. And others call it a roller coaster ride, with its emotional peaks and valleys. It is often a time of angst and self-doubt: Was I wise to leave a full-time job and return to school? I'm so young and lacking in experience. I'm so much older than the others.

In the spring of 2002, I presented my Education and Schooling students with this challenge for their summative assignment: "Who were you last August, and who are you now?" I invited them to describe their development as a five-stage process. Here's how one of them, Kelly Ann Smith, responded (reproduced here with consent):

Anticipation

In August, I was anticipating coming to Nipissing University. When I arrived on the first day, I was relieved to find someone I knew. Then we were split into sections, and I was thrust into a world of strangers. I resolved to get to know people and to have a good time; nobody knew who I was here, and there was no past by which to judge me. I greatly anticipated my practice teaching placements, although I thought that there wasn't much I needed to know, because I had some practical experience, and that would get me far. At the beginning of Education and Schooling, I was asked why I wanted to become a teacher. I could not articulate an answer which was satisfactory to me.

Disillusionment

Drawing my life map in this course was a disappointment. I didn't look ready to become a teacher. And just who was I, thinking I could become a teacher? Towards the end of my first placement, standing in front of the class, with a supply teacher in charge, I almost walked out of the class, with no intention of coming back. The students did not listen to me, even though I thought they would, I thought I could 'handle' them. After an incident with a student that day, I had a discussion with the principal. I was beginning to realize how much I did not know, how much I needed to learn. During this placement, I would come home tired – disillusioned that teaching was not for me. I felt I could not handle coming home every night, feeling so tired, still having to plan, still having to mark, and not feeling that I had accomplished any teaching during the day, only controlling the chaos, not even 'managing' the students' behavior.

Confrontation

During my first placement, I was confronted with an awkward situation that I helped to create; it involved an incident with a student. I had backed a student into a corner, leaving him nowhere to go, and he lashed out at me. I was stunned, and barely able to control my emotions. After talking with the principal, this not being the first time I had talked with her, I was feeling discouraged. But I needed that 'dressing down' to ground me, to rid me of the illusions I was holding onto about myself, my teaching abilities, and my knowledge of teaching. I needed to be humbled. This incident had been building, with this student and with others in the class. They were testing their limits with me, and I had reacted strongly, but not in the best way. In my reflection, an assignment for this course, but an exercise I would have done for myself regarding this incident, I confronted some things about myself that I had been denying or ignoring.

Competence

During my second placement, I was beginning to feel that I could teach, not just manage, a class. A student, new to the school, who had an IEP being written, was having difficulty. My first raw reaction was to let him be. Upon reflection, I realized that I was not respecting the intellectual diversity of my classroom. When I took the time to give him extra help, he was able to complete the assignment in a satisfactory manner. I had to look beyond my own personal bias and reach out to this student to help him to succeed. It was most satisfying for both the student and for me. I received daily satisfaction from the students, who were interested in and motivated by what I had planned for them.

I received constructive feedback from my associate teacher during the first week, which I incorporated into the lessons that followed. The continuing feedback reflected a growing competence on my part. I was actually growing and internalizing suggestions and improving my teaching and planning skills as the weeks progressed. As the placement proceeded, there was less feedback about things that needed to be improved, and more on the things I was doing well or had improved upon.

Culmination

At the end of my second placement, in conference with my associate, I expressed frustration with what I considered the overwhelming task of covering so many curriculum expectations. I felt I had only covered very few. My associate pulled out the curriculum document and proved to me that I had actually covered quite a few, and that a lot of curriculum expectations are covered incidentally, in the course of everyday teaching. I was beginning to realize that I could be a teacher. My life map, constructed in September, did help me towards my career in teaching. I realize now that I still have much to learn. This internship process will continue into my career as a teacher. I can see now how it will apply to at least my first year of teaching, if not more. I have learned that personal reflection is an important component in my own personal growth. It is a practice I intend to continue. My education as a teacher is not finished when I walk across the stage to receive my B.Ed. degree. It will already be my second degree. I have so much more to learn; even in the last two weeks of classes, I am still learning. I realize that I can now answer the question about why I want to be a teacher. I want to help students to discover the wonders of the world, to be able to communicate their own wonder and excitement, to help understand themselves, to help them to make their way in the world, to create a secure place in their lives. I have developed my philosophy of education to the point where I have a good grasp of it. I can identify the philosophies of others and decide whether I agree and, if I do, whether I can incorporate them. I was placed with an associate teacher who had a similar philosophy; it was interesting to see

> *it in action. I reflected on my observations, looking for ways I could improve my teaching and incorporate some of my associate's practices. Is there light at the end of the B.Ed. tunnel? We are not passengers on a train in the B.Ed. program, hurtling at great speeds to some predetermined station where we all get off at the same end place. We are on a journey on foot, divergent in our past, converging for the present, diverging again at the end. We can see all around us, behind us, about us, beside us and, more importantly, ahead of us. We decide when the journey ends. The B.Ed. program is only part of the journey upon which we have decided to embark. The rest is up to us. I am ready to continue my learning journey. I have matured, learned, grown. I am ready for adventure, challenges, and change.*

I was astounded that this B.Ed. candidate, who had seemed so confident in class, had "almost walked out of class, with no intention of coming back." But I also noticed that she had switched, in her narrative, from describing her students as "the class" or "a class" to laying claim to them as "my classroom." She had developed the framework for a personal philosophy of education. This person who had started out thinking "that there wasn't much I needed to know" now believed that she had "so much more to learn." By the end of the program, she was able to confidently answer the question, "Why do you want to be a teacher?" She believed in herself as "a teacher." (In 1998, as the References for this chapter indicate, she described her own research into the B.Ed. journey.)

I too was on a journey. After almost thirty years as a teacher, administrator, and consultant, I was a beginning teacher educator. A chance encounter with a publisher's catalog introduced me to Sweitzer and King's (1999) notion of a five-stage journey:

> ANTICIPATION (What if?): excitement; anxiety; normal doubts or worries such as "Have I made the wrong decision?"; "What if I can't do this?"; "What if I have a difficult class?"; "What if I don't get along with my associate teacher?"; "Am I a student or a teacher?"; "How will I juggle the demands of this program with my other responsibilities?"

DISILLUSIONMENT (What's wrong?): a time when the candidate is not as certain or positive about the placement as s/he would like to be. The candidate may not be looking forward to the day ahead, may muttering to him/herself or grumble to friends. Feelings of frustration, anger, sadness, disappointment, and discouragement are normal. So is sleep deprivation.

CONFRONTATION: instead of quitting or denying that there are problems with 'you', this entails facing and studying what is happening to you and "moving through" it, by reflecting critically on the situation and making plans to get out of the swamp. Candidates will know that they are through this stage when they feel more independent, more effective and more empowered as a learner.

COMPETENCE: with more competence, the candidate's excitement and accomplishments will grow. Morale and trust are usually high, and the candidate is beginning to feel like a professional (or 'think like a teacher'). A candidate who strives for perfection, rather than excellence, will likely face stress from (or in) his/her non-teaching life.

CULMINATION: as the year ends, candidates experience pride in their achievements and sadness that it's over. They reflect on their future education plans, on friends and family and relationships. There may be feelings of emptiness, of guilt or unfinished business if this stage isn't celebrated.

I applied this theory in my practice, and found that it was useful. I examined other theories of teacher development. White (1989) applied the anthropological notion of "rites of passage" to preservice teachers, arguing that they go through three stages: separation, the acquisition of specialized knowledge, and a ritualized return to the community. Similarly, Modiano (1975) suggested that some Aboriginal educators may experience three stages: chaotic (a sense of mismatch between traditional, informal teaching and the formal education structure); cookbook (adopting the formal methods demonstrated to them); and reconstruction (integrating some aspects of formal schooling back into their culturally valued processes of learning). Brown and Moffat (1999) discuss the mythic hero's spiral of growth from naïveté to self-awareness. Like legendary heroes who set out on a dangerous journey from the safety of home, slaying dragons as they seek the grail, heroic teachers follow six stages: the loss of innocence; chaos and complexity; the vision quest; encounters with companion-helpers; trials and tests; leading, at last, to insight and transformation. Others describe a developmental process for preservice teachers that is not linear, but "a complex process of extended and ambiguous 'in-betweenness'" involving multiple rites of passage (McNamara, Roberts, Basit and Brown 2002).

From my experience with an assignment in my first Education and Schooling classes, I am convinced that it is vitally important for B. Ed. candidates to understand that they are on a 'journey', to know that their highs, and especially their low points, are probably normal. I now teach them about the B. Ed. journey, and I recommend that they monitor their growth in a journal, recognize the natural stages of this journey, and not be overly concerned if their journey isn't a smooth one, or if one week (or placement or assignment) seems worse than the last. I advise them to fasten their seatbelts and enjoy the ride.

References

Brown, John L. and Cerylle A. Moffett. 1999. *The hero's journey: how educators can transform schools and improve learning*. Alexandria VA: Association for Supervision and Curriculum Development.

Canada. *Statutes by Title <http://www.e-laws.gov.on.ca/index.html>* accessed 7 March 2008.

Long, John S. *Welcome to Educ 4102*. *<http://www.nipissingu.ca/faculty/johnlo/thinklikeateacher>* accessed 7 March 2008.

McNamara, Olwen, Lorna Roberts, Tehmina N. Basit and Tony Brown. 2002. *Rites of passage in initial teacher training: ritual, performance, ordeal and Numeracy Skills Test*. British Educational Research Journal 28,6: 863-78.

Modiano, Nancy. 1975. *Using native instructional patterns for teacher training: a Chiapas experiment*. Proceedings of the first Inter-American conference on bilingual education, Rudolph C. Troike and Nancy Modiano eds. Arlington: Center for Applied Linguistics.

Ontario. E-Laws Website. *<http://www.e-laws.gov.on.ca/index.html>* accessed 7 March 2008.

Ontario College of Teachers Website. *<http://www.oct.ca/>* accessed 7 March 2008.

Smith, Kelly Ann. 2008. *The journey of preservice teachers*. M.Ed. thesis, Nipissing University.

Sweitzer, H. Frederick and Mary A. King. 1999. *The successful internship: transformation and empowerment*. Pacific Grove CA: Brooks/Cole Publishing Co.

White, J. 1989. *Student teaching as a rite of passage*. Anthropology and Education Quarterly 20: 177-95.

Balancing the Teaching of Math Education:

Understanding of Self, Problem-Solving, and The Need to Survive as a Preservice Teacher

Mike McCabe

Throughout the twelve years that I have had the pleasure of teaching mathematics to preservice teachers, I have questioned the efficacy and structure of our formal education system. My eight years as a parent have reaffirmed my beliefs of its current structure.

The structure of educating all students with the same content in the same manner at the same age level leaves much to be desired, and ultimately reinforces the idea of an "average" student. Our assessment strategies are geared toward mediocrity, and reinforce this ideology.

The acquisition of problem posing and problem solving skills, central to current and future intellectual development, often get stymied in the name of testing. Teachers become conditioned to teach to the test, and students respond by regurgitating testable content.

I openly recognize my personal bias regarding the failures of the schooling system. While teaching, I attempt to balance these with the reality facing my students once they enter their own classrooms. Central to my role as a teacher educator are the following components:

1. Attempting to challenge the teacher candidates to interpret their experiences in mathematics, and how these will influence their approach to teaching it. In doing so, I hope to challenge them to question and appreciate their abilities.
2. Modeling the development of problem solving skills inherent in the doing of mathematics, and to relate these to real life situations.
3. Directly responding to the teacher candidates' desire to understand "How do I teach [enter math related concept here]."

Personal Experience

Recognizing that preservice teachers come to a Faculty of Education with a wide range of ability, experience, and past successes, I attempt to take a practical (lived experience) problem posing and solving approach in the courses that I teach. Each teacher candidate has the opportunity to share her or his successes (and struggles) and the strategies they used in dealing them within the subject disciplines. This sharing creates the basis for further development, and teaching of a number of strategies. As the "resident expert", I see my role as one that recognizes the strategies and relates them to the subject areas and beyond. It is the acquisition of these strategies that assist learners in becoming confident, and in recognizing the areas in which they excel.

As adults and future teachers, our students should become adept at recognizing and sharing their expertise with others. In doing so, I attempt to link their successes to some aspects of the collective curriculae, and to emphasize to the teacher candidates that the curriculum content associated with the subjects we teach is simply the vehicle used to provide children the opportunity to experience success. In order to provide the opportunity for success, one must begin to question and adapt the content.

I battle an on-going conflict between my personal philosophy on education and that which appears to dominate the formal schooling culture: namely assessment and evaluation. It is my experience that, too often, teachers are consumed with the content of the curriculum and the role of assessment (i.e., pressures from administration, community, EQAO testing result) rather than the purpose of education. I do all I can to model a supportive, productive environment that downplays the importance of achieving the "norms". Restated, I recognize that our students will be responsible for the assessment and evaluation of their students, and I feel somewhat obliged to introduce them to some strategies to do so; but at the same time, I attempt to open their views to a world where the growth of individual children is celebrated, rather than the comparing one child's achievements to others or to "norms".

The teacher candidates we teach are all university graduates who have the ability to learn content: they have a lifetime of doing so (and quite successfully). What is different in a Bachelor of Education is teaching the learners to step back from the content to understand why we teach it, and what strategies we may adopt to provide children with the opportunity to succeed. Also, within this paradigm, I attempt to disengage teachers from the notion of a "best teaching practice" and replace it with several strategies that attempt to breed success in their learners. Understandably, teachers use personal experience as first reference for learning. They tend to teach how they were taught, and best understand learning how they learned. I see it as my primary task to introduce them to alternative strategies and stimulate growth by asking them to use the newly introduced strategies, and by challenging them to become comfortable in learning and teaching these strategies. I liken it to hearing a remake of a classic song for the first time (e.g., a Beatles classic redone by a more contemporary band). It takes a number of times of listening to the new versions before the listener can begin to accept it. The new band is not asking that we forget the original version; they ask only that we accept the remake and sing along.

Problem Solving

Problem solving means engaging in a task for which the solution method is not known in advance. In order to find a solution, students must draw on their knowledge, and through this process, they will often develop new mathematical understandings. Solving problems is not only a goal of learning mathematics, but also a major means of doing so (NCTM, 2000).

The mathematics curriculum aims to challenge all students by including expectations that require them to use higher-order thinking skills, and to make connections between related mathematical concepts and between mathematics, other disciplines, and the real world (Ontario Mathematics Curriculum, p. 3). Reference to "real world" is made no fewer than fifteen times in the curriculum.

Still, there appears to be a prevailing sentiment that there is disconnect between school mathematics and the mathematics necessary for success in the adult world (school vs. real life math). McCulloch-Vinson (1997) concluded that both teachers' and students' unfavorable feelings toward mathematics centred around the lack of emphasis placed upon understanding, teaching that is detached from real life experiences, and paper-and-pencil drills. They encouraged an emphasis of learning with manipulatives and authentic learning situations that mimic mature situations of dealing with mathematics.

Although there is a direct connection between the problem solving strategies developed within the curriculum and real life situations, I argue that the connection is largely implied – that we as educators seldom recognize or directly transfer the learned strategies from mathematics to real life situations. Within my course, I spend considerable time attempting to do so.

In an effort to make the implied problem solving strategies more overt, I often begin by using the analogy of experiencing a flat tire on a deserted country road and pose the question, "What would you do?" For each solution the students present, I offer another barrier, *i.e.* if students suggest using a cell phone to call a tow truck, I respond, "we are in a dead zone with no signal for cell phones"; if they suggest changing the tire, I create the barrier of "no available spare tire in the trunk". After many options and an equal number of additional barriers, inevitable someone says that they would just sit and cry. I always respond "Now we are talking: welcome to the teaching profession!" The idea of having a number of strategies available to solve problems is then connected to the concepts of mathematics.

Taking the concept of connecting math to real life problem solving to a practical level, I provide the teacher candidates the opportunity to develop concepts for lessons based upon their (and children's) daily routines using math. I also model this with a "day in my life" as a math teacher, posing mathematical questions regarding everyday events and observations related to consumerism. These experiences are then linked to the curriculum in a problem posing manner.

One skill I attempt to enhance in the teacher candidate before they leave the B. Ed. program is their ability to question the curriculum and its underlying purposes. Of course, in doing so, they must understand the curriculum. Again, this relates to their abilities to make connections between the concepts presented in the math curriculum, real life and other curriculae in schools. We often go through the curriculum to identify areas of uncertainty in their minds. Inevitably, questions regarding assessment and evaluation are often presented by the teacher candidates. They are consumed (rightfully so) with their responsibility to accurately report on their students' abilities and progress. It is here that I become most unsettled, and attempt to present the previously mentioned balance between personal belief and the reality of the schooling system.

Teaching Mathematics

Anyone who has taught future teachers can easily identify their questions related to "how do I teach [enter any concept here]." To this end, a large component of my course deals with introducing strategies to assist teacher candidates in their direct teaching of mathematics concepts. In keeping with currently accepted pedagogical approaches in mathematics, "representations are necessary to students' understanding of mathematical concepts and relationships" (NCTM, 1989), the use of manipulative materials play an important role in developing the concepts in mathematics. For example, when introducing the concept of two-digit multiplication, there is the necessity for the prerequisite understanding of the concepts of multiplication developed through the use of manipulative materials, its use in our world, and the underlying algorithms of single digit multiplication. It is hoped that the introduction to a variety of representations will enhance teacher candidates' conceptual understanding and increase the number of strategies available to them when teaching their own students. The skills in completing calculations can then be practiced and reinforced as necessary. I introduce this method of teaching for each of the key concepts necessary to effectively teach. In doing so, I also provide a number of age-appropriate, real life examples of problems, along with access to a number of resources that could be introduced once the teacher candidates are in their own classrooms.

In addition, I introduce strategies to enable teachers to gain an understanding of what children know about mathematics (and what teachers can do to enhance this knowledge). Most of these strategies centre around students' communication – verbal and written – with their peers and with the teacher. Teachers should become adept at recognizing key elements that indicate understanding and at posing questions to enhance students' depth of response. It is reinforced throughout my course that these strategies are used to help the students succeed, not to evaluate them in meeting the demands of report cards.

Of course, time is the greatest limiting factor in my job. Creating a balance between what the teacher candidates want (resource and strategies) and what I feel should compliment this (self understanding and curriculum familiarity) is a challenge. I attempt to satisfy all requirements while maintaining a consistency of the main message related to posing and solving problems. I feel it is best undertaken through an understanding of what each person brings to the classroom, and building upon this to increase the opportunity for success.

References

McCulloch-Vinson, B. (1997). A comparison of preservice teachers' mathematics anxiety before and after a methods class emphasizing manipulatives. *Early Childhood Education Journal*, 29(2), 89-94.

National Council of Teachers of Mathematics. (2000). *Principles and Standards for School Mathematics*. Reston, VA

Ontario Ministry of Education. (1997). Ontario Mathematics Curriculum. Toronto, ON: Queen's Printer.

How to be an Effective Teacher of Senior English

Janet McIntosh

WHAT DOES IT MEAN TO BE A TEACHER OF ENGLISH? After teaching secondary English for thirteen years, I had definite ideas about what makes effective teachers of English. Three years ago, when I began to teach the senior English elective at Nipissing's Faculty of Education, I was in for both a surprise and a challenge. What I thought the preservice English teachers needed to know, they didn't seem to *want to know*. I felt it was important to begin with the theory behind the teaching of English, but many of them were anxious to gather strategies that could be used immediately on their practicum placements. Their interest seemed to be in acquiring a series of prepared lessons; building a theoretical base first, examining the content to be studied, and then introducing them to various strategies for classroom implementation was my approach. I believe that selecting strategies is based on informed decisions about which ones are the most appropriate; the *why* is as important as the *how*.

Balancing the theory and practice is a major issue in teacher education. The practice part is the focus for practicum placements, but I wanted to extend this practice into my course. Encouraging students to engage in some English classroom strategies in the course itself was one technique that I was intent on using. Preservice teachers would benefit from experiencing the strategies that they've read about and discussed in course work before they actually use them in classrooms. A theoretical base is necessary before a program can be created with carefully selected strategies. Opportunities to familiarize themselves with the Ontario Curriculum in English (grades 11 & 12) and to learn about the strands for English courses – Literature Studies and Reading, Writing, Language, Media Studies – would be provided throughout the course; implementing the required expectations is often the difficult part for novice teachers. I wondered, how would I meet their needs, but also prepare them for the realities of the classroom, and the demands of senior English teaching in the secondary school? After much reflection, as I have taught the course over the past few years, I've gradually been able to achieve what I believe is an appropriate balance between the theory and its practical application.

Four expectations serve as the focus for the senior English elective course. In my mind, theoretical understanding of pedagogy and subject matter is of utmost importance. Theory provides the basis for classroom practice; integration of theory and practice is necessary. Providing opportunities to acquire practical strategies with a theoretical basis is another expectation. Developing and articulating a theory of English teaching which will inform teachers' classroom practice is a third expectation. A final expectation is that of acquiring a current understanding of research in the field of language arts/English teaching.

Simply stating the expectations is quite straightforward, but providing opportunities for preservice teachers to reach them is the challenge. Course assignments are designed to assist students with meeting the four expectations.

The first assignment is the Triple-Entry Notebook. Students make entries in this notebook as they read, reflect, and discuss professional readings from a course pack that serves as the text. Senior English teaching texts and journals are the sources for this compilation. Readings include theories, contemporary issues of concern, and strategies for classroom practice.

The notebook's three parts include summary, personal reflection, and peer sharing. Student writers select readings, complete parts one and two independently, and during small group sharing, record peer comments in part three. Time for reflection on readings is beneficial for students. Writing about what they have read engages them with the text in a valuable way. Some class time is provided for reading and writing initial reactions; some class time is devoted to small group sharing of thoughts about the readings. Sometimes comments from peer groups are brought back to the whole group for discussion.

The opportunity for preservice teachers to become familiar with theories and strategies for teaching secondary English is provided through this assignment. Rather than the professor introducing a topic through a formal lesson, readings often serve as a stimulus for the class addressing a particular issue in high school English classrooms. The issues that students have a particular interest in are often highlighted through this process. Writing about what they've read gives students the chance to consider their own views before sharing them with others. Oral sharing assists students with clarifying their views by being exposed to the opinions of others; it also provides the chance to articulate views. Articulating a theory of English teaching helps students to internalize what they have learned; informing one's classroom practice is often the result.

The Triple Entry Notebook encompasses reading, writing, and oral activities. The combination is appropriate for English classrooms as these skills are focused on in the senior curriculum. Students see this activity as one they can modify and use themselves. Therefore, by engaging in this activity, they acquire a clearer sense of how and why they could employ it in their classrooms.

Assignment two involves the writing of a Reader Response Journal and participating in a literature group. During the initial class, students select one of five novels commonly taught in senior level English classes. Five or six students sign up for the novels in order to ensure that all five are examined, and that they can later share with peers who have read the same novel.

Over a two-month period, in class and outside of class time, they read five twenty-page segments, and keep a reader response journal with entries of about one page each. Entries are written as they read 100 pages of their selected novel. On predetermined dates, completed entries are shared for twenty minutes in their literature groups. This strategy models an approach students can use with their own English classes.

I've observed that students are actively engaged in the discussion of their novels. As teachers of English, they need to have an awareness of the essence of literature study; simply knowing the content of a novel isn't enough. Students in senior English often have some skill in reading, but analysis is emphasized at this level, especially in the university preparation courses. Sharing reactions to their reading assists them with delving into issues in the novels. Although the issues they discuss may not be the same as those discussed in Senior English classrooms, the process is similar. Not all high school English students are avid readers, but many are.

These literature groups provide the chance for students to move beyond the text; such engagement in the text allows them to critically examine their own reading experience. The act of reading can be modeled in the senior English course. One aspect of this activity allows preservice teachers to immerse themselves in an experience that their own students might have as they read. Involvement in the process is much more authentic than only discussion of it. The debriefing of this activity is valuable, as they often examine their multiple roles as readers, students, and novice teachers of English, and gain further insights into the importance of literature study.

Writing three lesson plans with a rationale is the culminating assignment. Students select literature (novel, short stories, plays, poems, or a combination thereof) at the senior English level, and create three lesson plans which form part of a curriculum unit. They also prepare a rationale on why they selected the literature and pedagogy. Requiring the students to demonstrate their knowledge of the English curriculum and the practical classroom applications appropriate to meet the expectations for a specific grade and destination is an integral part of this assignment.

Writing the rationale is challenging, as preservice English teachers must demonstrate their comprehension of both theory and practice. Although they will have created many lesson plans during the preservice program, they will have had infrequent opportunities to write about why they selected specific pedagogy and strategies for each lesson. Evidence of integration is expected within these lesson plans, as this assignment is the last one, completed in the final month of the course. By this time, preservice teachers will have a clearer sense of how theory informs practice in English teaching.

This assignment is an ideal one for demonstrating synthesis of many components of the senior English course. Current understanding of research in the field of high school English language arts teaching is acquired by preservice teachers through course readings I provide and sharing of my own research. The course pack is comprised of readings from various journals that focus on senior English teaching. This approach highlights current research, as practical strategies and theory are included.

Although preservice teachers are given a reference list of texts, the content can often be out of date by the time the texts are published. Exposing preservice teachers to professional journals allows them to familiarize themselves with titles in English teaching, and then consider which ones to access themselves when they leave the university setting. Life-long learning is a desired goal, and reading journals is the way many English teachers and educators – such as myself – keep constantly informed about theory and practice. When I've attended English education conferences, I've often shared experiences and new resources with the students upon my return to the senior English course.

Sharing my own research is another means of assisting preservice teachers with keeping up-to-date with current practice. In the past three years, I've conducted two studies on reader response journals, one focusing on preservice English teachers and the other on first year teachers of Language Arts/English. My research examines teachers' attitudes about implementing reader response journals, and the process they use to introduce them to language arts and English students. Discussing this work with preservice teachers provides them with insight into a current classroom strategy: I've discovered that they have a particular interest in asking questions about my research. They recognize that my enthusiasm for and commitment to a particular English teaching approach originates in the research I am conducting.

Becoming an effective teacher of English is a challenging pursuit. Reflecting on my expectations for preservice teachers, I recognize that a thirty-six-hour course is only the starting point. Developing one's 'teacher-self' occurs over an extended period of time, well beyond the limits of a one-year preservice program. Novice teachers continue to learn and grow in their early years of teaching. By seizing opportunities to practice what they've learned in the senior English course with students in their own classrooms, their understanding of English teaching is further enhanced. I've observed that preservice English teachers in the senior elective course are passionate about English, and the teaching of it. Personal commitment and dedication to the demands of teaching senior level English are strengthened through acquisition of a theoretical basis for teaching practice. As novice teachers embark on their careers, it is my hope that their enthusiasm for subject of English can be instilled in the students they teach; this is my own ultimate goal as I prepare them to become effective teachers of senior English.

Art Education for the Generalist Elementary Classroom Teacher

James A. Mroczkowski

Each year, as I reflect upon and intuitively sense the eager-to-learn and professionally-focused hearts and minds of a new 'batch' of young (and some not-so-young) teacher candidates, I reminisce upon my first year as a teacher educator. I recall my own innervations, to share and illuminate theory through the stories of my own collective educational experience. I'm sure that many teacher educators do this, but we don't seem to talk about it much, so this opportunity to briefly chronicle my tale as a professor of art education from the start of my career to the present is in itself an edifying experience.

In my first year in the Faculty of Education, I remember the way that I wanted to "tell them everything" about teaching art, and what I "knew" about it. I clearly recollect the enthusiastic energy I possessed, and the unrestrained excitement I embodied as I anticipated my upcoming classes. While I remember little of the actual preparation and planning that I must have done, I do recall teaching my classes with ease, and the sense of well-being I felt while in the midst of teaching. I remember thinking how I wanted my students to be inspired, moved, and invested in my topic at hand. More than anything else, I wanted to affect a dispositional shift in their attitudes about how teachers could and should teach art to young children and pre-adolescents.

I remember too, how I felt after teaching. Those post-instructional recollections were bracketed with feelings of pride and an unabashed awareness of personal accomplishment, coupled to frequent notions of uncertainty of my instructional effectiveness, in addition to the sense of readiness I held for the next teaching episode to repeat and augment the gains or to make up for the shortcomings of the last teaching event.

Little has changed over the ensuing years. I still get excited about the prospect of teaching a new cohort of teacher candidates. I still feel those 'butterflies in my stomach' as I step in front a new array of student faces. I still crave the variabilities of teaching as I continue to be fed by the avidity for learning brought into the classroom by my students. And, as such, I remain committed to demonstrating the best practices of teaching that I possess and can model before them.

Moreover, my educational goals remain essentially the same. I still strive to inspire, motivate, engage, and inform the next generation of teachers so that their students, in turn, receive the bettermost of my subject or discipline, and the necessary understanding and meaning of art education: that which is theoretically grounded, pragmatically based, and offers qualitative human experiences for young learners.

What has changed for my students and me is the quantitative content of my teaching. At one time I tried to teach them 'too much'. That is, I wanted them to acquire a great deal of disciplinary as well as pedagogical knowledge in far too short a period of time. The instructional hours of my course have not changed since I started teaching here. What has changed is my focus and emphasis of what is important to 'know' in teaching art as a beginning teacher.

My early thoughts held that teacher candidates needed to understand and accept that teaching art well required a highly specialized set of knowledge and skills. While having such aptness would be obviously advantageous, it is not a prerequisite for being an effective teacher of art to children as a classroom generalist. I explain to them that they "don't have to be a 'mathematician' to teach elementary school mathematics, nor do they have to be a 'scientist' to teach elementary school science . . . hence, you don't have to be an 'artist' to teach elementary school art." What they do have to be is "willing" to teach art as it should and can be taught – if they seek out the rich abundance of detailed and specific resources that are "out there" designed to assist classroom generalists in delivering high quality experiences in art education with children. So I stick to illuminating some basic concepts. I teach them some fundamental skills in planning art education experiences, and I address how the Ontario curriculum can be implemented. All of this understanding is tempered with the basic tenets and principles of contemporary art education theory.

Since the early 1980's, Disciplined-based Art Education curriculum or DBAE as it is better known (Clark et al, 1987) has been designed, prepared, and ready and available in a variety of instructional formats (text, video, cd-rom, etc.) to be used by teachers to achieve this aim. A DBAE model of art education is predicated upon the position that not all children are destined to become artists, craftspersons, or designers. However, this curriculum model is posited on the notion that everyone will be a 'consumer' of visual information and communication, and that through the acquisition of *visual literacy*, learners will be better able to construct meaning from their aesthetic experiences with art and design (Housen & Duke, 1998). The disciplinary substance of the DBAE model of art education is informed by the content emanating from four distinct but interdependent and related disciplines of: i) art production (i.e. making art), ii) art criticism (analyzing and evaluating art), iii) art history (learning about art), and iv) aesthetics (determining the nature and value of art). As such, it remains my ambition to instill an awareness in teacher candidates that art education for children involves more than 'just making things' that we may call 'art'. This awareness is achieved if they themselves have some experiences with what it means to become more visually literate. Consequently, my classes engage teacher candidates with a variety of positive, success-oriented, non-threatening, and constructive learning opportunities to look at, examine, study, research, question, discuss, as well as make 'art' (i.e. informed practice) in very much the same way that I would use with children (i.e. through teacher modeling). In addition, I attend to the pedagogical foundations of the instructional methods that I employ, and encourage the teacher candidates to investigate and discuss alternative means of accomplishing the same curricular expectations through different teaching approaches (i.e. reflective research). In combination, these two endeavors provide teacher candidates with "belief perspectives" (Chambers, et al 2001) that they too can do it themselves.

As a consequence of my own reflective practice as a teacher over time, I have reduced the volume of my course content, and have designed lessons that optimize, emphasize, and focus my energy on the affective domain of my students' learning. I know that if I can change their attitudes about 'how and what it means to teach art to children', I can take comfort in believing that they will eventually address this role and responsibility as classroom generalists with genuine concern for maintaining the integrity of the subject; that they will not marginalize it within the curriculum and the school timetable, as is often the case with teachers who truly do not understand its importance to the overall development of the learner.

I know how powerful the socializing forces are in shaping what teachers do in the classroom (Hoy & Rees, 1997). I am aware that the system (i.e. 'schooling') has a tendency to reproduce itself from one generation of teachers to the next (Zeichner & Gore, 1990). I also realize that we often teach the way we were taught, much like the way we tend to parent the way we were parented. In order to intervene in this cycle, to disrupt the continuity of it, and to enable new teachers to teach the subject well, I know that I have to alter their attitudes about art education and what it means for them to guide children towards heightened visual literacy. I also know that this aim can be achieved if they come to see art education as more than simply one activity after another which results in the regular production of thirty nearly identical artifacts being made, taken home, and stuck on the fridge.

Armed with a sense of efficacy and directed through my guidance to the available resources, I am confident that the teacher candidates who have successfully completed my course will provide genuine, meaningful, and authentic learning experiences in art education with children in their own classrooms. I am confident of this because they will possess the requisite attitudes and dispositions for 'doing it the way it should be done' and not simply teaching art education in the ways they were taught themselves.

References

Chambers, S. M., Henson, R. K., & Sienty, S. F. (2001). "Personality types and teaching efficacy as predictors of classroom control orientation in beginning teachers". Paper presented at the Annual Meeting of the Southwest Educational Research Association (24th, New Orleans, LA, February 1-3, 2001).

Clark, Gilbert A., Day, Michael D., & Greer, W. Dwayne. (1987). "Disciplined-based art education: Becoming students of art". *The Journal of Aesthetic Education*. 21(2) pp.129-193.

Housen, Abigail and Duke, Linda. (1998). "Responding to Alper: Re-presenting the MoMA studies on visual literacy and aesthetic development". *Visual Arts Research*. 24(1).

Hoy, W. K. and Rees, R. (1997) "The bureaucratic socialization of student teachers". *Journal of Teacher Education*. 28(1), pp. 23-26.

Zeichner, K. M. and Gore, J. M. (1990). "Teacher socialization" in W. Robert Houston (ed.) *The Handbook of Research in Teacher Education*. New York: MacMillan Publishing Co., 329-348.

Changing the Face of Physical Education

Barbara Olmstead

"Mens sana in corpore sano"

As educators, we continue to ignore this ancient maxim: "a sound mind in a sound body." Now more than ever, these words echo through the halls and into the gymnasium. Today's teachers face additional challenges in their classrooms; almost 30% of their students are overweight or obese, children are being diagnosed with type II diabetes in record numbers, and for many students, physical inactivity has become the lifestyle norm at early stages of childhood development. In this climate of increased accountability for academic achievement, the marginalization of physical and health education will have lifelong consequences far beyond grade scores on standardized tests. It is within this environment that I continue my crusade to impress upon our future teachers the equal importance of physical and health education in the overall education of their students. In the few short contact hours with our Education students, my goal is to instill in them a sense of urgency. Indeed, this emergency situation requires immediate and ongoing care.

My job is to prepare our prospective teachers to feel comfortable taking their students to the gymnasium, so that Physical Education becomes an important part of every school day, and not an inconvenience or a privilege to be withdrawn at the whim of the teacher. It is a continuing source of frustration and disappointment for me to hear that teachers still hold PE ransom as a classroom management strategy. Physical Education, just as any other subject, is a students' right, not a privilege. My first lesson includes asking my teacher candidates to swear an oath, which states, "I promise never to withdraw physical education class for poorly behaving students." I have no way to enforce this, but it is my hope that our graduates uphold this ideal.

Let the Games begin!

All of my students enter the gym on Day One as experienced physical education students. At that point, however; the similarity ends. For many, the sight of a hardwood floor with painted lines often evokes fear and trepidation, not to mention anxiety. This is compounded by the thought that they may actually have to lead a PE class! I am very hopeful that no matter how permanent their predispositions to this anxiety, my experiential approach to Physical Education classes will induce a quieter state, and thus, a mind open to the possibilities that exist in a most dynamic, enriching environment.

I have an expectation that all students participate to the best of their abilities, and very seldom does this present a problem. In fact, I have to continually remind students that they are no longer sixteen years old, and that perhaps they cannot move quite as quickly or nimbly as they once could!

One of the biggest challenges for students is to make the transition from student-participant to teacher-participant. Because of the diversity of students in the Faculty of Education, the variety of skills and abilities is perhaps most noticeable when students express themselves through physical movement. The competitive mindset of many must be replaced with one characterized by cooperation, consideration of others, and teaching applicability. This is a difficult transition for those students who have enjoyed positive experiences in sport and physical education. These students just want to play, often getting caught up in the moment. Those students who have had negative experiences in physical education would rather just stay out of the way! This dichotomous situation (not unlike a typical elementary PE class) presents many challenges, but at the same time, creates relevant learning experiences.

Heightening awareness of varying ability levels in a PE class is critical in planning an inclusive program that recognizes diversity across multiple domains. Placing limits on my students hopefully gives them a greater sense of understanding of this principle. A carefully planned pause in the action with a guiding question or two encourages teacher candidates to consider various ways to modify the activity to enhance inclusion of all students. Physical Education class is often the only opportunity for youth to engage in physical activity during the day. An inviting environment that allows students to participate in a developmentally appropriate program free of judgment is the first step toward enhancing healthy active lifestyles. This must ultimately be the overriding goal of Physical Education programs in schools. I take every opportunity to model and promote this goal in each class.

As Shaw once said, "we do not stop playing because we grow old, we grow old because we stop playing". Many Faculty of Education students are not unlike elementary school children: they love to play! For some, however, the desire to play has been suppressed in adulthood. My challenge is to rekindle that desire, so that my students are willing to try everything. In my view, experiential learning best prepares our students to create safe, positive, inviting learning environments for their students. They are more likely to retain many of the activities presented if they themselves have engaged in them as participants. Multiple opportunities to interact with others in different ways afford a greater range of options available to teachers. Each class is fast-paced and active. My students are challenged physically and cognitively to become competent

Physical Education teachers. In the brief time I have with them, I cannot expect complete transformations; but I hope that I can begin that process!

To encourage lifestyle adoption of physical activity, Physical Education teachers must be creative. No longer can we rely on the old standards of basketball and volleyball alone to maintain interest. While these two continue to be popular for most PE programs, I feel we must broaden our curricula to include activities that can be lifelong pursuits. There are so many competing options in the lives of our youth that teachers must be entertainers; they must be prepared to sell their product to their clients! Providing a program of variety will contribute to and sustain interest in Physical Education, hopefully resulting in enhanced participation for a lifetime.

I am not suggesting that skateboarding or hang gliding become compulsory activities, nor should teachers provide a different activity each day. But a 'repackaging' of Physical Education programs may embrace the interests of more students, particularly those at greatest risk. Successful teachers are able to anticipate these interests. They recognize that not all of their students will love volleyball, and while volleyball may be an excellent activity that can be a lifelong pursuit, it may not provide all students with the opportunity to meet curricular expectations. More importantly, however; volleyball may not necessarily enhance the development of positive attitudes toward healthy active living. As an example, the use of pedometers in a walking program may provide a viable alternative to those students who do not excel at volleyball.

One critically important role of a Physical Educator, and too often ignored, is that of Health Educator. In particular, sexual health education is something I feel must be addressed in my classes. This topic is one that teachers hope parents will deal with, and parents hope teachers deal with it, and as a result, it does not get dealt with at all! Many teachers have good intentions: they include sexual health education in their long range planning. The problem is they relegate it to the end of the year, hoping it will just go away! In my view, sexual health education must play a more prominent role in the classroom. Anatomy and mechanics are straightforward, but I like to deal with the 'yucky' stuff : healthy relationships, decision making, and creating a trusting, open classroom environment that encourages students to ask the critical questions. I challenge my students to think about their personal attitudes and values, and the importance of remaining unbiased in their teaching.

I hope to impress upon my students the importance of their role in becoming advocates for Physical and Health Education. I encourage them to become enthusiastic role models for healthy active living. At the very least, I hope my students leave their teacher training year with the courage to try new things; the bravery to go beyond their comfort zone; the desire to seek new and interesting ways to present the curriculum to their students; and most importantly, the confidence in their abilities to influence young lives in a positive way.

Reflections on the Importance of the Purpose of Education & the Role of Teachers

Michael Parr

According to the Academic Calendar, the university Senate approved description of Education and Schooling reads as follows: Education and Schooling (thirty-six hours) is designed to enhance the knowledge, understanding, and skill of teacher-candidates in the area of the philosophical, historical, legal, and social contexts of schooling and education. Through readings, dialog, observation, seminars, and reflection, you will be encouraged to discover the multifaceted nature of modern classroom teaching and to discover and understand who you are as a 'teacher'. The intent of this course is thus to offer materials and experiences that develop a strong foundation for professional teaching.

Central to the Education & Schooling course are the questions of "who are you as a teacher" and what does a "strong foundation for professional teaching" consist of? Answers to these questions lie in historical and current paradigms that position teachers within a wide variety of political, social, legal and philosophical frameworks. Because each of these forces is fluid and ever-changing, we see that the answers to such questions are often elusive and dynamic: that is, they vary from person to person, time to time, and from one cultural, political, or geographical location to another. Rather than providing students with a definitive understanding of their roles and responsibilities as a teacher (because this role is ever-changing); it is more critical than ever that we empower teacher candidates with the understanding and skills required to individually make informed critical judgments that will guide them in the development of their own philosophy, sense of purpose, and overall understanding of their role as teacher.

To facilitate this, the Education and Schooling course presents an opportunity for students to explore three pillars that encompass historical trends in education, a variety of philosophical orientations that include but are not limited to: Perennialism, Essentialism, Progressivism, Existentialism, Humanism, Constructivism, and Social Reconstructionism; and legal responsibilities of teaching as defined through the Education Act, various Ministry Policies and Ontario College of Teachers Standards and Foundations for Professional Practice.

These portals may reflect the 'foundations' of teaching; however, we must go well beyond the basics in preparing our teachers for what lies ahead of them. To assist teachers in translating these foundational components into praxis, we explore a number of topics that facilitate integration, synthesis, and application of material being discussed to the challenges that teaching presents in the 21st century. Such topics include an examination of factors related to issues associated with diversity, multiculturalism, poverty, sexual orientation, early school leaving, gender, violence/bullying, and the like. Each of these topics is examined in light of our responsibilities as teachers in a legal sense, as guided by legislation, government policies (including Ministry of

Education Acts and Regulations, The United Nations Universal Declaration of Human Rights, The Canadian Charter of Rights and Freedoms, The Ontario Human Rights Code), and Board policies. Students are encouraged to explore their own understanding of such issues in consideration of their professional responsibilities as a teacher, and to define for themselves what they are called to do in response to the challenges before them. Recognizing that these are individual understandings, the course continues to challenge students to determine and define for themselves what their developing philosophy and ethical sense calls them to do.

In order to facilitate this growth, dissonance is often intentionally created in the hopes that teacher candidates will challenge their own understandings (including the need to maintain the status quo, and to address issues of equity, social justice, rights, freedoms, privileges and responsibilities) within society, as well as on a broader scale. Admittedly, some students remain comfortable and committed to the preservation and perpetuation of the myriad of hegemonic discourses that serve to justify action or inaction, and the very institutions and processes that maintain and perpetuate ideologies and the status quo. This too is a legitimate right of all persons. Again, these are individual discourses and individual choices which lead teacher candidates to ask themselves how far and how deep they are prepared to go to challenge and engage themselves as teachers of the 21st century. In turn, as teachers, each is called to exercise their responsibilities as they question, explore, analyze, and synthesise all that is before them in order to engage their own students in meaningful exercises and dialog around the world we live in: the world children in schools will inhabit long after we have departed this life.

In-class activities and discourse often produce more questions than answers for teacher candidates. This, however, can be a good thing if accompanied by the licence of empowerment: the tools of confidence and self-efficacy that will propel each candidate to think critically and to search out the answers to questions and challenges that we, as educators in the 21st century, are not yet equipped to acknowledge or address. We must acknowledge that life is full of uncertainties, for ourselves and our teacher candidates, as well as for the generation of students that they will be teaching over the next thirty years. What is critical, however, is how we will, individually and collectively, navigate through these uncertainties and meet the challenges that lie before us.

In the final class in my Education and Schooling course, I read to my students the classic book by the well-known philosopher Dr. Seuss, *Oh, The Places You'll Go!* It quite profoundly describes the journey we are all on, in life, in relationships and in our professions. It encourages us to look within, be true to ourselves, but be open to change in understanding, and in habit. Following the reading of the book, I share a few concluding remarks with students. It's the only time I read from a scripted text in class. It's the only time I intentionally share my own words of wisdom (whatever they are worth) with students.

I end here with the text of the message that I share with students at the close of the course, and invite anyone reading to take from it what resonates with you: whatever may, in some small way enhance your own understanding of self, teacher, or of what it means to be fully human, alive, and an active participant in this wondrous experience of life.

Final Message: The Journey Continues

It has only been seven months since you began the teacher education program,
You're not that much older, but different.
You're not students any longer . . . you are very soon to be Teachers . . . Real Teachers.

So what does that mean to be a teacher?
Being a teacher implies a certain level of status, prestige, and responsibility.
You are in a very privileged position of power and influence over our most valuable assets,
That is, over the most impressionable members of society, our children and youth.

It's an awesome responsibility . . . being a teacher,
But a wonderfully exciting and powerful opportunity as well.

The question we ask today at the closing of this course is,
"What does it mean to be a teacher?"
Have your views changed since September,
when you began this program?
Do you have a clearer understanding of what your role as a teacher is?
Of what the purpose(s) of education is/are?
Do you have a clearer sense of the political, social & economic forces
that make the role of the teacher and the purposes of education
such contested questions?
Is it all clear to you now . . . what it means to be a teacher?
I would expect not. It always has, and will remain contested terrain.

I recognize however that you are all thinking well beyond the teaching
of the basics; reading, writing, and numeracy.
These are only subject matters through which we teach the actual
lessons of life,
The essence of what it means to be fully human,
How to think, to act, and to live compassionately, with respect for our
fellow human beings.
That is what you teach and model each and every day.
Much more than the basics of academics,
In reality . . . you are teaching the curriculum of life.

And what does this curriculum include, and who determines this?
Do you now know what knowledge, skills, and values you are supposed
to, or want to 'transmit' to your students?
Alternatively, which values, biases, prejudices, and stereotypes that
you want to break apart and reconstruct with your students . . .
is it even transmission of your/others' values you want?
Or do you want to transform?
To have students construct meaning and define for themselves,
to engage and empower your students, to challenge them to become
self directed, self motivated, problem solvers,

Students who can reflect on their lives and the world around them and think critically for themselves,
Students who can effectively embrace the challenges we have before us?

Today you are a student here within the faculty,
But tomorrow you are a leader.
You will lead through example, as teachers and as models for your own students,
Who in turn will grow up and shape the country and the world we live in. In reflecting upon this, Henry Adams said it best:
"A teacher affects eternity . . . she can never know where her influence stops."
What an awesome responsibility that is: to shape the world of tomorrow,
the imprint of which will be felt long after you are gone.
What a legacy . . . what a responsibility.

This is a great world we live in.
From some privileged vantage points, it's a great time to live,
But it can get better for a great many more people throughout this world.
And it is up to us to collectively do our individual parts to make this happen.
As teachers you are poised to have much influence in this regard.
And with that influence comes responsibility.

As teachers, we have the responsibility to empower youth to change the world in which we live in positive ways and in response to the many challenges they will face in a future world that we can hardly envision at this time.
You will be the catalyst for them to do this.
You will be the model, the 'significant other', the spark that ignites the flame, the catalyst for transformational change that in subtle, and possibly in several not so subtle ways, fundamentally alters the world in which your own children and grandchildren will grow up.

This is quite a responsibility,
quite an honor,
to be a teacher in today's world,
as there is now more opportunity, and more responsibility than
ever before.

To meet these challenges, I encourage you to continue to grow
as teachers.
Continue to be critically reflective,
In the way you conceptualize the world around you,
In the way you see your role as a teacher,
And in your understanding of what teaching practice is all about.

I encourage you to set high ideals and standards,
For yourself as well as your students
And not to allow yourself to get discouraged over your setbacks,
Because there will be many . . .
Recognize that there is seldom only one way, one view in teaching, or in
life,
And that our students are entitled to travel many paths, not just the
ones upon which we ourselves have travelled.
Recognize then that accepting and even embracing diversity and
alternatives bring opportunities for growth and development,
both personal and professional,
And that such challenges to our way of thinking are opportunities
to expand our own world view, and that they allow us to change
the lenses through which we see the world.
Such opportunities allow us to redefine our perspective from time
to time: to grow,
and are to be embraced and celebrated, rather than shied away from.

You have an exciting future that awaits you as a teacher.
Make the most of it, finding a balance between friends/family,
students/career, and "ongoing professional learning" . . . 'reflect' lots.
Although most of you recognize that you still have so much to learn,
and that we have barely even glimpsed the tip of the iceberg

regarding all the knowledge and skills you will develop as a teacher over the years,
Rest assured that your year at the faculty here has indeed prepared you well,
For whatever teaching placements you find yourself in,
And hopefully to some extent for whatever else might lie ahead of you in your lives.

In the next few years, as you rise to your challenges, you yourselves will learn to further refine your skills as critical thinkers, as well organized, efficient teachers,
As flexible and adaptable, self directed, self motivated, problem solvers,
Who feel engaged, and hopefully, now at the end of this course,
Empowered to make a difference:
A difference in the lives of the students you will teach,
A difference in the schools within which you teach,
A difference in the communities that you select to settle in.
And in doing all of this . . .
A difference in the world in which we all live, today, tomorrow, and for many future generations to come.

My final comments to teacher candidates, as well as to readers of this text, are that in closing, I suggest we make this difference through our everyday interactions with others, one simple act at a time . . . each and every day, through each and every step we take in concert with others . . . in essence: one starfish at a time.

THE STARFISH *Once upon a time there was a wise man who used to go to the ocean to do his writing. He had a habit of walking on the beach before he began his work. One day, he was walking along the shore. As he looked down the beach, he saw a human figure heading toward him, moving like a dancer. He smiled to himself to think of someone who would dance to the day.*

As he got closer, he saw that it was a young man, and the young man wasn't dancing, but instead he was reaching down to the shore, picking up something, and very gently tossing it into the ocean.

He called out, "Good morning! What are you doing?"

The young man paused, looked up, and replied, "Throwing starfish in the ocean."

The older man then asked: "Why are you throwing starfish in the ocean?"

"Well, the sun is up and the tide is going out, and if I don't throw them in, they'll die."

"But young man, don't you realize that there are miles and miles of beach and starfish all along it. You can't possibly make a difference!"

The young man listened politely, then bent down, picked up another starfish, gently tossed it into the ocean, past the breaking waves, and said:

"Well sir, it made a difference to that one . . . "

(Author unknown)

Just Like Frederick:

Literacy Journeys into Another Time, Another Place

Michelann Parr

August 14, 2006

I READ *THE TIME TRAVELLER'S WIFE* by Audrey Niffenegger this past summer, and thoroughly enjoyed it. As I conceptualized this tale that I had been asked to recount and rehearsed it in my mind, I saw the possibility of using the structure of time-travelling to help me recall past literacy experiences that have shaped who I am as a literate being today and, therefore, how I teach. Here I am reminded of the words of Meyer (1996) who boldly stated that "you are who you teach and you teach who you are" (p. 3).

As I sat down to write, I realized that I was so immersed in the story and so lost in the lives of the characters that I had actually forgotten their names. I can now remember their names: Henry and Clare. I first recall thinking that time-travelling was such a gift for Henry until I realized that he did not have the benefit of any of these memories. He was unable to recall the experiences granted to him through time-

travelling, and unable to control the place to where he was going or the time to which he was travelling. His journeys were not sequential, and the story did not begin at the beginning, nor did it really end at the end, not for Henry anyway. It seemed that in the end, he was doomed to a life of time-travelling, virtually alone. So, in that sense, I realized what a curse time-travelling actually was for him.

Then I considered Clare's point of view and applied the same logic. What a gift for her to know that someday, somewhere she would meet the love of her life: and he loved her so much that he time travelled back to prepare her for the life that she was going to assume. A gift to be sure, in that she knew she was loved out there in time and space somewhere . . . but a curse in that she lived her life in waiting. Her lived experience was a waiting experience: waiting for Henry to time travel back to see her, waiting to see him in real time, waiting for her memories and experiences to come true in real time so that she could share them with him, waiting for him to leave her, and then, even in knowing that he would never again be with her in real time, waiting for what was a memory of the future to become present and for him to leave her yet again (Unpublished Reader Response, 2006).

As I began to construct and plan my tale, I realized that I had a significant advantage over the lived experiences of both Henry and Clare. I was in a position to bring forward memories, reconstruct stories, and share fully who I am as a teacher and as a learner. For me, time travelling would be a virtual state of mind that would enable me to move in and out of memories as they fit my conceptualization of who I am as a literacy learner and an educator of literacy. As I sat thinking that a good place to begin would be now, with a description of what I currently do and who I currently am, I found myself gently whisked away to another time, another place.

October 4, 2005

I was given a book today, Parker Palmer's *The Courage to Teach*, which helped me to understand what it is I wanted to achieve for my students in my language and literacy course. I could speak to you here about the formal course expectations listed on my course outline, or the more specific characteristics of effective literacy teachers described by the International Reading Association, but I won't. Instead I will discuss the three paths that I want my students to explore in my course: the intellectual, emotional, and spiritual dimensions of language, literacy, and literature.

> *By spiritual I mean the diverse ways we answer the heart's longing to be connected with the largeness of life – a longing that animates love and work, especially the work called teaching. By intellectual I mean the way we think about teaching and learning – the form and content of our concepts of how people know and learn, of the nature of our students and our subjects. By emotional I mean the way we and our students feel as we teach and learn – feelings that can either enlarge or diminish the exchange between us (Palmer, 1998, p.5).*

When I think of language and literacy, I think of possibilities that extend beyond the simple mastery and application of theory, strategy, and technique. I think of communication, connectedness, and lived experience. I think of the emotional dimension of teaching, which links us to the worlds of our students and the reciprocal journey upon which we embark. I think of language and literacy as forces that enable us to make connections within ourselves, texts, others, and the world. I think of language and literacy as an interdependent and socially constructed process, as opposed to an independent, autonomous product. Rarely do I separate language and literacy from experience – experience provides a support, a scaffold, and a way of understanding language, which is often composed of texts and words. Even less often, do I separate language and literacy from literature – literature provides a powerful image, a relevant metaphor, and a shared experience . . . literature helps us to illustrate our words, unearth buried messages, and make sense of an otherwise confusing world.

May 2, 2004

How very odd! I am walking through a Casino at the base of our hotel. As it turns out, Reno, Nevada is the site of this year's International Reading Association Conference. What an unlikely place to gather thousands of reading teachers! I stroll through the casino; the memory of last night's entertainment was sharp in my mind as I decided to gamble $20.00 and only $20.00. Today I could laugh! After the first four slot machines, I win nothing. Not a single coin makes its way into the tray at the bottom of my white bucket.

I peer anxiously into my white bucket, which holds perhaps five remaining tokens. And that's when I notice someone walking behind me from machine to machine, pushing the button . . . you know, the magic button that returns any winnings to you. I return to the slot machine and insert my token, finding the button.

One by one, two by two, I make back my $20.00, and that's when I decide to stop . . . but that's also when I realize that the lesson I had learned was far more valuable than any winning I could have possibly put in my pocket. I learned that regardless of how literate we are, there are always situations that will render us illiterate; some might argue 'unskilled or inexperienced', but I assure you, I felt completely illiterate. Not only that, but I realized the embarrassment of many who struggle with literacy on a day-to-day basis. What a powerful story this would be to share with my students!

I'm still shaking my head as I walk into the convention centre, straight through to the Reading Market Place. I love books, and I especially love the challenge of bringing back books as souvenirs that capture the essence of my travels. I enjoy the little ones that contain inspirational poems or stories that I can relate to or use as energizers in the classroom.

As I always do prior to purchasing, I open the book. It is entitled *Life's Literacy Lessons*, written by Steven Layne (2001). Immediately, I find the poem *Another Time, Another Place*. This poem describes the author's desperate need to take his readers to another time and another place . . . through the pages worn and tattered, and the tales we need to hear, he leads us on a search that knows no end, a search that leads us through other lives to live, different pasts, and different journeys.

How exciting to have found this poem. It is how I feel about reading: some days I find myself transported away, living the life of another, experiencing their feelings, simply lost in a story. Yes, the poem refers to children, but at the end of my second year at the Faculty of Education, I realized that adults, especially developing teachers, deserve the experience of being transported to another time and another place as well. Some of this they would do through exposure to well-selected literature on my part. And some of this they would need to do on their own as they revisited times and places that influenced who they are as literate beings and who they will become as literacy educators.

Preservice teachers enter our classrooms from many different times and places which have led them to delight and wonder, terror and fear, tragedy and care (Layne, 2001). Not much different than a regular classroom, they enter the faculty of education as a diverse group of learners with various strengths, abilities, and needs. It is our role, as teacher educators, to take them from where they are to where they can ultimately be (Clay, 1985); it is our job to lead them on a journey from readers and writers to language and literacy teachers. These journeys do not initiate within a faculty of education, but awareness of their implications often does. It is a necessary beginning to engage preservice teachers in an investigation of who they currently are as language and literacy users, and where they have come from. Even more critical is their reflection on how this will shape who they will become as language and literacy teachers of the future. Language and literacy is a place where past, present, and future are often inextricably linked, a space where intellectual, emotional, and spiritual paths are often intertwined and unpredictable.

July 15, 2006

I am staring at last year's course outline, trying to determine what I want to keep and what I want to set aside. I made many changes last year, but am still not entirely satisfied with it. I'm not sure that I am getting at the heart of who my students are in a way that enables them to build a schema or structure to organize new information with. The literacy autobiographies I had them do last year were very heavily slanted toward reading, despite the fact that I believe that at the heart of literacy lies Frederick (Lionni, 1967), with his immense power to use words to transform the world. A tiny field mouse, Frederick was able to gather sunrays for cold and dark winter days, colors to keep the grayness of winter at bay, and words and tales to pass the time in the long winter days. Frederick's voice, as if magic, had the power to transform the world of his comrades. I decided then that the literacy journeys that students were going to embark on this year should be multifaceted, and should deal with listening, speaking, writing, viewing, and representing, not just reading.

Just as they did last year, students would need to revisit their literacy past and identify key experiences, key memories, and often key texts. They would explore their previous lives as listeners, speakers, readers, writers, viewers, and representers, taking stock of attitudes and beliefs for further investigation, and making way for new ways of thinking about language, literacy, and literature. This clearing of space is critical if we are to participate intellectually, emotionally, and spiritually in the development of young readers and writers.

> *It requires that we get our hands dirty and remove the overgrown weeds and dirt clods of our lives, knowing we may receive a few ant bites in the process. We must each reflect on our own journey as a [literacy learner] if we want to be the best guide we can be for those who will depend on us for assistance. In doing this, we will be wiser and more attuned to what lies before us as teachers, opening up a wealth of possibilities for seeing our lives from a new perspective - through the eyes of young [literacy learners] (Glover, 1999, p. 7).*

An in-depth understanding of literacy learners that extends beyond observation and interviewing is critical; teachers are far more effective if they have a sense of what it actually feels like to be a reader and a writer, what it really means to feel illiterate. They need to understand what students are saying when they say, "I can't write a story, I can't figure out that word", or "it makes me really nervous to share my ideas." Often, this understanding comes from struggling through the writing process, puzzling through word solving in reading, or developing the confidence necessary to be an active speaker and representer. My driving belief is that we should never ask students to do something we are not willing to do or have not previously tried; engaging in tasks similar to those required of our students breeds understanding from their perspective and their viewpoint. One of the most powerful learning opportunities I provide to my preservice teachers, therefore, is that of experience in activities similar to those that they will plan and implement with their students and intensive reflection on the process. Johanne vonGoethe's quote is a prominent one in my course:

> *Knowing is not enough; we must apply.*
> *Willing is not enough; we must do.*

May 15, 1996

I'm not sure whether this was the first time that I met Frederick, or whether I had encountered him in previous lives . . . what I do know is that this is the strongest memory I have of him. Frederick, a little field mouse, perceived as a lazy daydreamer, is misunderstood by his peers. Frederick though, knew better. He understood the power of language and literacy, and had the capability to use language and words in a powerful and unique way.

I'm sitting on the carpet in the corner of my classroom, reading Frederick to a group of Grade 1 students. We are discussing the unique gifts that we each have. Some of us are listeners, some orators, some readers, some writers, some mathematicians, some scientists;

each has a gift to be celebrated. As I listen to these Grade 1 students, I marvel at their acceptance of individual difference, as they call out eagerly, "Yeah, like Matthew is really good at making us laugh!" or "Jack always helps me when I can't figure out a word." Our discussion is lively and enlightening, and as I put Frederick back on the shelf, I realize that his is a story that needs to be told over and over again, to children, to parents, and to teachers.

September 15, 2007

I read Frederick to my students every year, usually as we begin our segment on literacy . . . what I want to share with my students is the immense power of language, literacy, and literature to transform our lives, as well as the lives of our students. As well, I want them to understand that doing is not simply multi-dimensional in terms of learning style and multiple intelligence, but it is often multi-levelled in terms of engagement, which is often misunderstood by teachers.

Like Frederick, I want my students to gather sunrays, colors, and words to create and transform their own worlds, and the worlds of their students and colleagues. I want my preservice teachers to understand that they will have Fredericks in their classrooms, and that they must provide multiple opportunities for success for these students. I want my students to understand students like Frederick through their struggles and their literacy pasts. When my students leave my course, I want them to understand that teaching language, literacy, and literatures is far more than teaching about texts and words; it is about broadening students' world views in a way that helps them to fully participate and envision a world that is different because they live in it.

May 1, 2008

I returned today, to my window overlooking a rocky ledge with a pool of water deep below: I feel the warmth, I see the colors, and I'm searching for the story. I find myself writing in the dark again, both literally and figuratively (as van Manen, 2002, would say), wondering whether we write to understand or share our thoughts with others, realizing that writing is a huge leap of faith, realizing as my students do that a blank screen is pretty scary. Will others find interesting what I have to say? Is it worth saying? Do my words have the power to transform? As these words appear on my screen, I realize that I have come full circle, and that despite the fact that I have my memories, I am really not in a different place than Henry was. My story did not begin at the beginning, nor did it really end at the end, and maybe it never will. The difference though between his story and my story is that mine has the power to transform the life that I am living as a literacy educator and a literacy teacher, and this is what I truly want for my students.

I realizing that I am calling forward my past and present (perhaps future?) lived experiences in much the same way that my students will. I have perhaps hit a spot where the paths have joined and are merging together, although not for long, I'm sure. The intellectual path keeps me reading, researching, making sense, and writing to understand best practice. The emotional path keeps me wondering: How much struggle do you share with students? How do you share passion, enthusiasm, and love of language, literacy, and literature with students? And then there is the spiritual path, which keeps us grounded in the world around us. Will the telling of my story make a difference in the lives of my students? In the lives of their students? In the lives of other educators?

Galeano's (1988, p. 121) words resound in my mind, reminding me that struggle is at the root of learning and at the root of becoming:

> *We are what we do, especially what we do to change what we are:*
> *our identity resides in action and in struggle.*

And as I sit, waiting for the magical ending to write itself onto my computer screen, I realize just as Clare did that we can never fully envision the ending . . . we can spend our lives waiting patiently, or like Frederick, we can live them fully, re-visioning and transforming the world with sunrays, colors, and words!

And this is truly what I want to share with my students.

References

Clay, M. (1985). *The early detection of reading difficulties*, 3rd Ed. Auckland, New Zealand: Heinemann.

Glover, M. K. (1999). *A garden of poets: Poetry writing in the elementary classroom*. U.S.A.: National Council of Teachers of English.

Layne, S.L. (2001). *Life's literacy lessons: Poems for teachers*. Newark, DE: International Reading Association.

Lionni, L. (1967) *Frederick*. New York, NY: Alfred Knopf Books for Children.

Meyer, R.J. (1996). *Stories from the heart: Teachers and students researching their literacy lives*. Mahwah, NJ: Lawrence Erlbaum Associates, Inc., Publishers.

Niffenegger, A. (2003). *The time traveller's wife*. Orlando, FL: Harcourt, Inc.

van Manen, M. (2002). *Writing in the dark: Phenomenological studies in interpretive inquiry*. London, ON: Althouse Press.

Teaching Music Education

Sandra Reid

When I was first offered the position of teaching general music to Junior/Intermediate preservice teachers, I began a list of what I felt were the most important skills and knowledge that student teachers would require to successfully teach music in a classroom. I also asked many of my teaching colleagues what they felt should be taught in my future classes, and added to my list. Next, I researched and read several armloads of texts written on teaching music in faculties of education. With a pen in hand, I added what the theorists said to my list. This was a wonderful, comprehensive list of skills and knowledge from researchers and practitioners – about two hundred things to teach – in only twenty-four hours!

Realizing this impossibility, I tried to prioritize and list the top twenty skills in the hopes of planning my sessions around these 'essentials'. My background in Kodaly music curriculum training, doctoral courses in arts curriculum, thesis, research papers, and writing of music curriculum for school boards had given me much experience in sequencing the skills, knowledge, and concepts in music. Starting with the familiar songs, teaching pitches, and then moving on to beats and rhythms have been my mind set. Prepare some songs, isolate the new learning or concept from the known song, and lead students to understanding through specific questions. Reinforce the new learning: look for it in other songs. Practice the new concept by singing, writing, playing, and moving. Finally, assess the students' learning of the new concept.

After my first year teaching music in the faculty of education, I realized that my list of twenty 'essentials' to teaching elementary music needed to be reduced to two! If any of tomorrow's teachers are going to share the magic of music with their future classrooms of children, they need to do these two things really well. Firstly, it is not the key understanding of musical concepts, knowledge or musical skills that is the priority, but experiencing the joy of making music and realizing music's value!

Many adults have a great fear of music: it is a phobia that has been allowed to develop. Unfortunately, teachers and parents have often been the cause of this fear. Many students were told to 'mouth the words' when their class was performing in concerts. Some have been told not to sing by their parents or spouse. Many have not even had the experience of music classes while they were in elementary school. Since one must be successful in every subject in our program, I have had students who could not physically sit down in class on their first day without considerable effort and anxiety. Coming into the music room, many move directly for the very back seats in the classroom and hope that I will not notice them.

It is very important to get everyone involved making music initially, i.e. using peer pressure to participate before they are even aware they are making music. This is much the same approach that must be used as a grade seven or eight classroom music teacher when students have not had much music background in their primary and junior grades. I begin by teaching them a game song by rote, so we are making music and laughing from the start. They are not overwhelmed with symbols and concepts, but just enjoy the community that is their section or class. This also goes a long way in helping to create a comfortable class environment, where they understand that they will not be embarrassed, that everyone works together, that it is alright to make mistakes, that we will practice to improve, and that music is fun. This is the first 'essential' to learning to teach music, and it relates to our personal philosophy and to our planned curriculum.

‘Practice’ and ‘play’ are words often connected with the subject of music. It is the joy of play that helps keep us young, and can be a connector between student and teacher, as well as student and students. As we learn more songs, look at the concepts within the songs, practice and reinforce the concepts, students can read four pitches on the treble staff, hear the pitches and write a four bar composition using these notes. Team effort and team work/play are part of every class. There are many ‘aha’ moments when students start to understand the symbols in music and practice reading, writing, and creating music.

At this stage, we progress from our known notes and take a risk in learning a new instrument. I expect students to read and play at least five pitches on a recorder or keyboard, or three chords on a guitar. Students work independently and in small groups while I circulate and coach/assist. There is great joy when we share a concert of the class and for the class, after about five or six hours playing a new instrument. Student teachers are just as excited as if they were performing on stage at the Air Canada Centre! There is such a sense of support and accomplishment. Self esteem is so important to young adolescents - and to beginning teachers. It is in the moments like this that they have the feeling that they would like to share this experience with their own students.

Once student teachers understand the need to share music with their future students, they realize that they need specific music resources. At first, student teachers believe that all necessary and supporting resources, such as we have in our university classroom, are available in any school. Once student teachers have been in their first practicum, student teachers realize that not all Ontario schools are well supplied with texts, instruments, CD players, charts, and a well trained itinerant music teacher.

Each year of my career, I have added to this list of resources: finding out what works from other music teachers, journals, workshops, and conferences. Initially, this list was printed on a page and given to students within the course outline.

Eventually, I make a CD of student teachers singing songs done in our university class, as well as provided readings, computer printed folks songs, and a the list of music teaching resources suitable for Junior/Intermediate students.

After a decade of teaching music to both general classroom teachers and instrumental music teachers, my important 'list' of what essential 'things' to teach remains constant: to enjoy music, and to know where to find music resources suitable for young adolescents.

The Democratic Teacher

Carlo Ricci

Let us take, for example, the practice of cooking. Cooking presupposes certain kinds of knowledge regarding the use of the cooking stove. How to light it. How to turn the heat up and down. How to deal with the possibility of fire. How to balance the ingredients in harmonious and pleasing synthesis. With practice newcomers to the kitchen will confirm some of the things they already know, correct others that they do not know so well, and gradually open up the way to become good cooks.
(Freire 29)

GOOD MORNING, AND WELCOME to the Nipissing teacher education program. I would like to start off apologizing for my lengthy one sided dissemination of information today, and assure you that this is not going to be typical. There are several introductory things we need to get through. I would like to start off introducing myself, and presenting my political bias to you.

As most of you know, my name is Carlo Ricci, and I teach the Curriculum Development Assessment and Evaluation course. This course is divided into three parts: in the first section, we are going to examine various orientations to education; in the second section, we are going to examine how to create a unit; and in the third section, we are going to examine assessment and evaluation.

I will give you more detail on each of the three sections in a minute, but before I do I want to share with you my vision of education, and how it differs from what we currently have in Ontario. My primary theoretical influences are critical pedagogy and holistic education. In Ontario, the predominant educational orientation is an essentialist approach to education. A critical pedagogue is interested in what Paulo Freire calls "right thinking". In *Pedagogy of Freedom,* Freire tells us that part of "right thinking" is to decidedly reject any and every form of discrimination. "Preconceptions of race, class, or sex offend the essence of human dignity, and constitute a radical negation of democracy" (41). As a critical pedagogue, I am interested in the amelioration of society by giving those who have traditionally been oppressed and silenced a voice. The goal is to transform injustices within the status quo, and empower those who have traditionally been disempowered.

A holistic educator argues that "The aim of education should include the development of the whole person: intellect, emotions, body and spirit" (Miller vi). Instead, Miller goes on to argue that the schools are focusing on a few skills that can be tested [the essentialist model] and the price that we are paying for this narrow vision is huge.

As a critical pedagogue, I argue that the standardized curriculum we have in Ontario is undemocratic. I look forward to dialoguing with you about this throughout the year, but for now I just want you to consider the undemocratic nature of creating a curriculum that is standardized in a democratic society that should make difference its goal, not standardization. Put another way, if we value democracy, we need to value difference, and not standardization. Furthermore, the government introduced a grade 10 literacy test that all students need to pass before they can graduate from high school. The end result in many cases is that many teachers are pressured to teach to the test. And many students who do not fit the standardized model of learning will not get their high school diploma, and therefore will have their future options severely limited.

I realize that what I am doing is unfair. I am giving you all of this information without giving you a chance to respond. Let me stop and ask for questions or comments.

Student 1:

I agree with what you are saying, and I am glad that in this class we are going to address substantive issues, and not merely be trained into the status quo. I see this as the difference between education and training. Education gets us to critically reflect on the status quo, whereas training just tells us what it is and provides us information in how to work it more efficiently. I am looking forward to the rest of the year.

Carlo Ricci:

Thank you.

Student 2:

I disagree with what you are saying. I have two points. First, I am paying to learn how to become a teacher in Ontario, and at the end of this program I want to feel confident in working within the system. I want to be trained. Second, Carlo, you are against standardized testing, right? How else can we ensure that we are competitive in the global market?

Carlo Ricci:

You raise some interesting concerns; hopefully, we can continue to discuss throughout the year. For now, I will offer a brief response, and look forward to a continuing dialog. In response to your first point, by reflecting critically on what is expected of us in Ontario, we will inevitably gain a deeper understanding of what the curricular expectations are like in Ontario. In response to your second point, I think you are absolutely right in having us think about what the purpose of education is. Are teachers mere commissars of the capitalistic system? Do we work for IBM, Walmart, and other big corporations? Are we willing to reduce our jobs to teaching our students how to become better workers, thereby replacing the nation state with the corporate state? Or should education be about something more?

Once again, my political bias is as a critical pedagogue and a holistic educator. This means that I believe in democracy. I believe that we need to educate our students with the goal of the amelioration of society and the individual. We cannot reduce human beings to a limited set of skills that they can be tested on. For example, we cannot ignore our spiritual side that is fed through the arts, and we know that we are doing just that: cutting out the arts and, in the process, our soul in favour of the corporate nation.

Before I conclude, I would like to briefly outline how this course fits into my philosophy. First, I cannot stress how important it is for us to remember that education is not neutral, but political. In the first unit, we will be looking at various theoretical orientations to teaching. By exploring various orientations, it will be easier to see that how we teach in Ontario is not neutral, but politically charged. Given that there are other orientations, changing those in power can lead to the adoption of one of the other orientations.

Our second unit is on units. We will examine how we are expected to do them in Ontario, discuss what orientation this belongs to, and critically reflect on its merits and limitations. As well, we will discuss how other orientations treat the creation of units. And finally, we will look at assessment and evaluation, once again, critically reflecting on its merits and limitations. Of course, as teachers we do not neatly fit into a particular orientation, and this will be discussed as well.

In conclusion, teaching is an art; and like all good artists, teachers need to define their teaching from within. As a preservice teacher educator, my goal is to empower you and provide you with the information you need to critically reflect on what you are expected to do. As preservice teachers, you need to be made to feel empowered and in control. You need to be given the opportunity to feel human, and in turn to interact with your students as human beings. All too often, teachers and students pass each other in the halls without acknowledging each others' presence – without validating each others' existence. We need to learn to listen and to talk with our students, and not merely talk *to* our students. Learning takes place in a community of learners, in which the teacher is a member of that community. The teacher needs to assure the students that she or he is also learning within the community. In order for this to happen, teachers and students need to engage in what Freire calls problem posing education. They need to talk about substantive issues and deal with genuine problems. I would like to offer a series of comments that students have made about my teaching. I do this not out of narcissistic pleasure or self aggrandizement, but to show the impact we as teachers can have when we connect to others on a human level. As a human being, this connection is our greatest gift:

> *Dr Ricci,*
>
> *WOW! You made my day! Thank you so much for the encouraging feedback! It's ALWAYS nice to receive feedback, but it's ESPECIALLY lifting when you aren't sure if your presentation went over well!!! I hope that ALL preservice teachers will model themselves in your likeness – I know I will certainly strive to do so!!! . . . You are an example to us all! Thanks again for the lift!*
>
> *Melanie Blanchette*
>
> *I enjoy your class because it is so different from all of my other courses. You actually do what you profess to believe in and not all profs do. Thanks for a great class.*
>
> *Andrea Laidlaw*
>
> *Again, thank you for making my first evaluation so encouraging and "non-terrifying."*
>
> *Robin McKay*

Contrary to our current practice, teaching is not an externally imposed recipe, but it must come from within. And each of us needs to discover the teacher within.

At this point, you expect, usually,
general principles, rules.
But teaching is a practice. It is
Personal experience.
Teaching is a discipline that
Comes from within. Not one
That has been forced on you from
*Outside.**

* *I have borrowed Frédéric Leboyer's text, and replaced the word "birthing" with "teacher". This is from his book* Inner Beauty, Inner Light

References

Blanchette, Melanie. "Re: Presentation Feedback." E-mail to Carlo Ricci. 28 January 2003.

Freire, Paulo. *Pedagogy of Freedom*. Trans. Patrick Clarke. Boston: Rowan & Littlefield Publishers, Inc., 1998.

Laidlaw, Andrea. "Re: Presentation." E-mail to Carlo Ricci. 5 December 2002.

Leboyer, Frédérick. *Inner Beauty, Inner Light*. New York: Knopf, 1978.

McKay, Robin. "Request from Robin McKay." E-mail to Carlo Ricci. 3 February 2003.

Miller, John (Jack) P. and Nakagawa, Yoshiharu, eds. *Nurturing Our Wholeness: Perspectives on Spirituality in Education*. Rutland, VT USA: The Foundation for Educational Renewal, 2002.

Tuning Our Souls: Celebrating the Courage to Sing Our Own Songs

Carole Richardson

THOUGH MYRIAD ART FORMS nurture our soul and provide us with great pleasure, as a musician and preservice music educator, I have also had considerable experience in dealing with anxiety and self-doubt. As a singer and choral conductor, I have experienced it personally, and as an educator, I see it manifested in my preservice music classroom at the beginning of every term. To offset this, I have, in recent years, begun to welcome new students into my classroom by saying, "Good morning, welcome to music class. You will not, at any point in this class, be asked to play or sing by yourself". The broad smiles, lowered shoulders, expelled breaths, and smatterings of relieved laughter offered in response to this opening serve to highlight the ongoing anxiety that many teachers associate with bringing music into a classroom.

Music is often perceived as an area in which one either does or does not have talent. Few other subject areas grapple with this false dichotomy. People may perceive that they are not 'good' at math, but it is rarely expressed in terms of talent. As educators, we need to stop telling ourselves and others that only those with perceived 'talent' in music should teach or engage with it. Many students have shared privately that they have been asked, at some point, to just "mouth the words" when singing, but none have ever reported being asked to pretend they are doing addition and subtraction.

As with any discipline, very few people reach the pinnacle; but in music, those who do are very visible. Though not professional musicians themselves, many preservice and inservice teachers tend to measure themselves by this standard when, in reality, the opportunity to enjoy music, make music, and listen to music is every person's right. As teachers, we owe it to ourselves and to our students to take whatever knowledge and resources we have and offer our students an uplifting and interactive music programme. Though we are not all expert musicians, we are creative, dynamic beings; we are teachers.

In my experience, each preservice teacher brings an identity with them that relates to the role of music in their lives. We can deny these musical identities, but I believe that they will remain a part of the innate fabric of our souls and, at some point in our lives, these identities will find a way to emerge from the mental and emotional drawers in which they have patiently rested. They must be challenged and re-visioned within the context of engaging in joyful and authentic music-making in a safe environment in order to empower students to redefine themselves as educators willing to engage in creating the context for others to have authentic Arts experiences. What we bring to an experience initially determines what we take from it. As a researcher, artist and a teacher/professor, I have come to believe that music plays a part, some part, in every life; and until we ask ourselves what that is, we cannot be whole. To quote one of my preservice teachers, "Music is self-expression; it doesn't have to be perfect". We must create safe classroom environments where engaging in authentic and meaningful musical experiences is enriching for student and teacher alike.

Through my understanding of what music has wrought in my life – for I have, indeed, been shaped by and through music – I am able to bring musical ways of knowing to my classroom, to my research, and to my art. I do not compose, and hence do not 'create' Art in the same way that a visual artist or a composer or choreographer would. In this sense, I truly dwell in the borderlands of creation; I engage my artistry through interpretation and teaching as I create by re-creating. My art exists within a spiral of researcher, singer, choral conductor, and teacher. Music is ever-present, but the context within which

I am creating through re-creation determines whether music is the melody, the harmony, or the accompaniment. In some way, it invariably enables me to connect to the musical self, however acknowledged or ignored, that lies in the souls of others. This is the gift that music has given me through its sometimes dormant and sometimes very active presence in my life: the ability to touch the lives of others; sometimes directly through music, and always because of the greater awareness of 'self' with which music has provided me. I understand and live my identity as authentic and multifaceted, my various roles embedded within and overlapping each other, with music as the *passacaglia* that simultaneously grounds and links the different aspects of my story and connects me with others. In this way, the music within me permeates all aspects of my life, including all aspects of my teaching. Through acknowledging my musical strengths and weaknesses, I am able to help others do the same, both musically and personally, in such as way as to help them envision themselves as potential teachers of music.

I have come to believe – through listening again and again to the voices that speak in my classroom – that our musical voices are linked directly to our souls; more specifically, to our spiritual centres, and as teachers, this is the place from which we must draw if we are to allow our students to see and understand who we really are as people, as artists, and as researchers, sharing collective and individual truths.

In his book *The Musician's Soul*, James Jordan, a musician and choral conductor, speaks of metaphorical "journeys" in his life that have led and will continue to lead him to his "centre" or "soul". Though he credits different people and experiences for beginning each journey, he maintains that, "All journeys, in whole or in part, are always the result of an acquired ability to quiet my self-clatter to try to hear my own unique voice" (Jordan, 1999, p. 11). He often returns to the concept of inner voice while searching for one's centre.

> *One's innermost spiritual seat, the place from which all musical impulse grows and is nourished, can only be accessed through time spent with oneself. Time for reflection. Time for listening to one's inner voice, which, when heard, speaks ultimate truth, which is then reflected in music. (Jordan, 1999, p. 21)*

In listening to people, we demonstrate to them and others that they are worth caring for and about, and in valuing the stories of their lives, we assure them that their voices sing for us and tell authentic and meaningful truths as they know them. In this way, the concept of voice is collaborative. As we do not have experiences which are free from the influence of others, our voices cannot speak authentically if we value only our own words. It is in the silences and the resonances amongst the harmony and the discord that we find parts of ourselves in the lives of others. In doing so, we rediscover the universality of lives lived, and the human need for song and story to share them. Van Manen (1986) speaks of the need to shake each child's hand as they enter and leave the classroom:

> *It may seem a cumbersome ritual to shake each child's hand twice each day, but the teacher who makes the effort touches each child. How easy it is, otherwise, to let days go by without being in touch with certain children. The quiet and "easy" child can remain untouched for quite some time. (p. 21)*

To relate this idea to ourselves, we can think of the image of *touching* in a symbolic, emotional manner. Just as children need to be touched, we, as teachers, teacher educators, researchers, preservice teachers, need to get in touch and stay in touch with ourselves if we want to be able to truly touch our students. We must find the artist voice that sings of life experience, and apply that artistry and the understanding gained from our re-creation of our artist selves to our classrooms. It is through first hearing and then listening to our authentic voices that we can begin to understand what it is we know within our classrooms. And it is so easy to let days (years, lifetimes) go by without being in touch with ourselves. In the tradition of portraiture, if we are to know our own truths when we hear them, we must pursue the silences: those within us, and those within others. As teachers, our voices are and must always be reciprocal. Even as we invite others to join us in enriching our lives through song and story, the voices of past collaborators will echo our invitation.

To value the voices of our students, we must listen carefully to their silence and their song. An important measure of a teacher is what she can tell you about her students – not their marks or behavior, but their lives. Who lives behind the faces that look at you expectantly at the beginning of each new day? What are their challenges and their strengths, their fears, their joys, and most importantly, their dreams? After you have been teaching in your classroom for a while, pretend that someone has asked you to describe each child to them. What do you have to say about each of your students? Can you picture a face for every name? Do you know what their family situation is? Have you seen them sitting in the cafeteria? Are they alone or surrounded by friends? Do they have a lunch? Has anyone washed their clothes? Does anyone comb their hair? Have you watched; really watched as they come into your classroom? Do they stop and chat, or scurry so as to avoid hurtful comments and ill-placed attention? How do they react to your praise; to your displeasure? Do you know what interests them; what makes them happy, and what makes them sad? Do you find a way to praise equally throughout your class? Once you know what makes them smile, it's very easy to find the praise. Do you know why they sometimes raise their hands wanting eagerly to participate, while at other times avoiding your gaze? Do you know how they learn? Have you talked to or met their parents? What do you know about your students? Do you know your students? Is your classroom a place to learn and grow and share and take chances? If you think so, do you practice all of those things?

Look at the back of your classroom for the faces that try to stay in the background; meet their eyes and smile at them. Listen for the silences, and watch for those who work to stay in the shadows: be the one to notice them and to value them. If you are rebuffed, try again, and always leave the door open. Always endeavour to be authentic and kind. Everyone needs a little kindness in their lives. Your smile, your gentle word, the touch of your hand on their shoulder might be the only positive human contact they have all day. Value the voices of all of your students, and when you feel like shouting, look to laughter instead. Shouting makes us defensive, and laughter breaks through our defenses.

If, when you leave your classroom for the day, you know you have made an honest effort to value each child for who they are and for what they bring, that your classroom is a safe place, and that you have laughed with your students, then that is the definition of a successful day. Above all, forgive yourselves and your students daily for the mistakes you have made and will continue to make. We are all only human, and need to start each day just trying to do our best. Some days our best feels good enough, and others it doesn't. It's the trying that counts. Oh, and sing: sing with joy. As individuals, we might not need affirmation of the value of the arts in our lives, though reminders can be timely and welcome, but, collectively, as *educators*, perhaps we do. Preservice teachers must be reminded of and engaged by the uplifting, healing effects of participating in and reflecting on music-making within a community of learners/artists/preservice teachers as we collaborate to ensure that we are ready to help our students enrich and make meaning of their lives in and through music.

References

Jordan, M. (1999). *The Musician's Soul*. Chicago: GIA Publications.

Van Manen, M. (1986). *The tone of teaching*. Portsmouth, NH: Heineman.

What's so 'Special' About Special Education?

Warnie Richardson

In looking at several different approaches with respect to completing this narrative, I finally decided to deal with it as a year end speech, delivered to 192 of my Intermediate/Senior preservice student/teachers. It forced me to think about my course, and the year that was, from within the context of where we started from in September and where we ultimately ended up in April. Although it only speaks to one year in my teaching life, it identifies, without question, my general philosophy and specific priorities, as set within the parameters of both the profession as a whole, and my course, EDUC 4307: Special Education/Educational Psychology. This is what I had to say.

As I look back on the year that was, in a very non-linear kind of way, we have indeed covered a great deal of territory. Did we cover everything that was outlined in my "official" course outline, or perhaps was covered in the other divisions? Regrettably, we did not. For example, we did not discuss, in a great deal of detail, students with physical exceptionalities, students with hearing and vision challenges, and students with severe speech and language disorders. We barely scratched the surface with respect to those who are identified as gifted, and for that, I take full responsibility. I had every intention of getting to all the official designations that you will be required to teach in your fully integrated classrooms, but early on I recognized that in an eighteen week course, which is divided into two parts (with Educational Psychology and Special Education being equally treated) I could not do justice to the causes, to the exceptionalities, and most importantly to the students for whom you will be collectively programming, with approximately forty minutes devoted to each exceptionality. I have learned from experience that if I had approached all of these designations in the very rudimentary, superficial way that would have been primarily driven by severe time constraints, all I would have managed to do was perform one hell of a disservice to a specific group of students with some pretty profound exceptionalities, and scare the living hell out of you in the process, because I would have been forced to assign a great deal of reading without sufficient time to flesh out the intricacies of each official designation. For this reason, and this reason alone, I made a strategic decision. Early on, I knew that, given my particular teaching style and with my propensity for utilizing case histories (story telling), that time was going to be a factor; it always is with me. Thus, I made the decision to bump what I refer to as "high incidence" exceptionalities to the front end of my course, and "low incidence" exceptionalities to the back end of my course, knowing full well that I might run out of time, with, of course, quite resultant consequences.

As the course eventually played out, I probably devoted too much time to the underachieving, at risk, marginalized, resilient, behaviorally maladjusted, delinquent and learning disabled student, and did indeed run out of time. However, in looking back, I note that several other factors also came into play with respect to my allocation of time. On two separate occasions, once after coming back from your first observation week, and then again after your first official practice teaching session, I took the greatest part of two full periods to debrief; to talk to you about your individual teaching experiences in a very personal kind of way, particularly your "special educational" experiences. We talked about real kids in real life kinds of situations, and collectively we were able to offer some really useful and very practical programming solutions. We talked about things like Irlen Syndrome, Intermittent Explosive Disorder, Trichotillomania,

Selective Mutism, Crystal Methamphetamine Addiction, and Self-Abusive and Eating Disorders, not because they were delineated in my course outline or on a "special educational" document emanating from the Ministry of Education itself, but because they were areas of exceptionality that were deemed very important to you, as several of you were dealing with these types of extraordinary situations in your current regular or core classrooms. If I could completely have my way, I would design each class like those, and would rarely, if ever, refer to a textbook definition with a textbook solution. Because – as you will have learned by now, after having been in your own classrooms for over ten weeks – rarely, if ever does the same programming solution apply to the same designated exceptionality. For example, the learning disabled student who has been identified as having a "back-end" vision-motor integration problem and/or dysgraphia, but has also been diagnosed with comorbid "attention deficit" difficulties and Tourette Syndrome, will have very little in common with the learning disabled student who has "front-end" auditory processing and/or reading difficulties (dyslexia), but is also on medication for acute depression. The same holds true for the "behaviorally" designated student who may bring with him or her a long and very disturbing history of social maladjustment directly related to years of neglect and abuse, when contrasted to his or her "behavioral" counterpart who has a been diagnosed with a very specific mental health condition, like a Conduct Disorder or an Oppositional Defiant Disorder. In fact, as you have been made aware of while taking this course, there is some very real debate around the education of the affluent student when juxtaposed to his intellectual equal from a government housing project.

Another factor for which I take full responsibility is the way in which the class presentation component was run. I do not regret designing the course around sixteen very specific "educational psychology" theories, themes or issues but again, I suspect, I could have been more conscious of time. But first let me deal with the theories, themes or issues themselves. My thinking in designing this particular Educational Psychology/Special Education course was to look at specific theorists and theories, or general themes or issues emanating from these theorists and their theories (Steiner, Piaget, Havighurst, Skinner, Erikson, Bandura, Kohlberg, Vygotsky, Maslow, Bronfenbrenner, Gardner, Goleman, etc.) so we could, at minimum, briefly see how children should/could be developing in a somewhat universal or collective way. In my view, this overall approach then better enabled us to look at deviations within this general developmental/theoretical perspective, which basically goes a very long way in explaining the evolution of the "special education" student. The only question for me, when I was in the early stages of designing this course, was either to personally tailor my lessons around these sixteen theories, themes or issues, assigning readings, and then deploying a straight lecturing format; or assign the theories, themes and issues to you, have you research and present them, and then allow myself some time to provide some personal input as well. Of course, this is now all history, and we certainly know the design that I ultimately opted for: you doing the basic research and putting together the presentation, with me augmenting and facilitating your efforts where possible. With respect to this overall format, I certainly knew that my personal input on each of these themes or issues was going to be somewhat problematic, potentially, again putting some pressure on time, but what I was not prepared for, was the amount of work that you folks put into the development and delivery of each presentation, and the very well reasoned and articulate debate which immediately followed each presentation. As a result, very early on in the year, I had to make another strategic decision, to both limit debate and discussion, or let it flourish, to see where it eventually ended up. Knowing me as you now know me, this was a complete non-issue for me, as every class seemed to uncover another example of a "teachable moment": which I was so fond of bringing to your attention. Anyway, with reference to the course as a whole, regardless of the logic or illogic, the ups or the downs, the good or the bad, the impersonal or the personal, the intangible or the tangible, here we are coming out on the other side . . . we made it!

But what have we really made? Do we have all of the answers with respect to identifying and programming for the exceptional student? In short, we certainly do not! But if you have learned anything in this class this year, it is to be very suspicious of anyone who claims that they have all the answers, particularly those of the "quick fix" variety! Special Education in and of itself is like a multi-runged ladder, and with this particular course, we have merely climbed the first rung. Keep in mind that you are regular or core classroom teachers, and not Special Education Specialists or Resource personnel. This is not to say that you will not be someday; however, as we speak, there are other people functioning in these positions, and it is fundamentally their jobs to totally support you. Thus, at this particular point in your career, if I could give you one piece of Special Education advice, it would be this: If you do not like what you see, particularly related to the educational history of a particular student verses current performance in your class, do not just ask lots of questions, but demand lots of answers. If your gut tells you there is something wrong, in the majority of instances it has been my experience to find then there is indeed something wrong. Do some digging, do some documenting, even entertain some well intentioned speculating, then demand that someone prove you wrong. You have nothing to lose, but the student in question has so very much to gain.

With respect to managing behavior, always remember that inappropriate behavior is merely a symptom. If you do not take the time to try and figure out what is actually driving the bad behavior, you will only be managing the behavior, and this can make for a very long year. Keep in mind that most of the things that constantly drive someone to consistently act out receive their genesis outside of the classroom and indeed, even the school, so be prepared for what you might find: it can take you to strange and not always pleasant places. But again, I feel very strongly that, as teachers, we should always be prepared to take this journey with some of our "neediest" students because, in the end, you may be the only adult in their lives that is willing to do so. If research within the risk/resiliency domain has taught us anything at all, it is that most children, if they are to truly become everything that they are capable of becoming (their potential), will need to come into contact with at least one significant, caring, supportive adult, who, at some point in their developing years provides a degree of hope with direct reference to the future (of the potentially pleasant things to come). So please, I ask of you, do not hesitate in becoming that significant, caring, supportive adult!

When it comes to content, well, I need to clarify something. A while back, I made the comment that you could train a monkey to teach content, and that only incompetents run for cover under the content/curriculum umbrella. Without question, my assessment and commentary in this regard was a tad simplistic, and certainly not reflective of the full range of research that has been generated within this particular area.

It was and still is, however, an accurate appraisal of my practical experience in that, over the last seven years, I have received 106 urgent requests for help while you people were out practice-teaching, with not one of these urgent requests having to do with what it is you are required to teach. Lots of questions on motivation, lots on specific types of identified exceptionality, lots on underachievement, lots on integration and inclusion, and a whole bunch on the management of inappropriate behavior, but not one single request having to do with three digit multiplication, the use of nouns, verbs, and adjectives in the construction of a complete sentence, none on Canada's involvement in the Boer War, and absolutely none on the periodic table and/or photosynthesis.

But please, do not misunderstand me. Of course I believe there should be standards, constant evaluation and clear content guidelines. However, none of these should exist at the expense of all other potential educational gains. For example, if I was evaluating a straight up senior History lesson on the Holocaust, delivered to university-bound students, I would certainly want you to closely scrutinize the actual events related to this terrible event; however, I would also think that it would be a completely missed opportunity if you failed to speak to other issues such as racism, sexual orientation, and perhaps even the current situation in the Middle East, Rwanda, Sudan, or Northern Ireland. Hell, I would even think it was a missed opportunity if you did not supplement a lesson of this nature with a tune from Warren Zevon, Billy Bragg, the Sex Pistols or the Pogues . . . I know what you're thinking, the Sex Pistols and the Holocaust, what gives? Needless to say, it takes some effort, but I can tell you from experience that there is a pretty powerful lesson there!

These same general principals hold true within the broader Special Education context, perhaps even more so. It is my belief that learning, I mean real learning, can only take place when there is absolute engagement, and to get full engagement you have to nurture an interest. However, once this interest is revealed and mined, a relationship built on reciprocal trust is but a short step away. You will find, upon arriving at this particular juncture with a student – or group of students – even the most 'difficult' ones, that in measuring both behavioral and academic growth, you can move forward from here, most times, in truly remarkable ways! However, to be completely honest, there is one significant catch linked to this overall approach. To uncover an interest also demands that you devote some substantial time in just getting to know your students.

This is especially true of the underachieving, at-risk behavioral student, who may vehemently resist all initial attempts at relationship building, but I am here to tell you to "hang in there," as you may be the last adult in a particular student's life standing between him or her and who they ultimately become as adults. If it is not you, then it may be no one, and if it is no one, I am again here to tell you, based on personal experience, then the story is less likely to have the happiest of endings. For those students who most need teachers like you, I am asking you to work a little harder, to dig a little deeper, to hold on a little longer, as it just may be worth the effort! But be prepared, this general philosophy of mining interests and developing relationships can take you in many interesting directions, some of them perhaps not so popular with administration. Nonetheless, these battles can be won too, particularly if you absolutely believe in what it is you are trying to accomplish.

To conclude, with direct reference to *Special Education*, those whom I formally evaluate in a "practice teaching" capacity know that the two things that I value most highly are the ability to effectively respond to unpredictable situations, and the ability to take risks, particularly the risks involved in sometimes leaving the formal regimentation of your lesson plan. You will know that I absolutely love it when teachers take their students on a personal journey, one that has meaning and resonates within the individual and sometimes very troubled lives of those who make up the classroom. I think I consciously look for these characteristics in a teacher because I truly believe that these two ingredients are the most essential ones in the composition of the truly successful Special Education teacher. These are the teachers that students remember! They are certainly the teachers that I remember.

Speaking of the truly effective Special Education teacher, I mentioned earlier that they need to be constantly documenting, asking questions, demanding answers, and building personal relationships; but they also need the luxury of time. As I was very fond of saying throughout this academic year, there is not one aspect of Special Education, or the programming for children and adolescents who are functioning on the scholastic margins (the student at risk) which does not rely heavily on your ability to shut down Ministry driven educational expectations/applications, to effectively and completely deal with what makes these students so special or so exceptional in the first place. Interesting times to be a teacher!

In the end, what words of wisdom can I impart that might make your role as a regular classroom teacher a little clearer, perhaps even a little easier? Well, when everything is said and done, I really do not have any. In the end, for the most part, you must find your way, for the most part, on your own. Within yourself, within your own teaching style, you must find that judicious balance between compassion and harshness, between freedom and control, between curriculum and reality, between content and citizenship; in essence, the balance between creating the brilliant mathematician or historian and just a decent, moral, valued, caring human being. When you have done this, you will have become a truly exceptional teacher, one that can cover the content and curriculum, but also deal with the living and breathing entity that wants nothing more than to have a meaningful life beyond the four walls of your classroom. But this is all very easy for me to say standing up here, with no real or magic prescription on how to become this teacher.

If I was left to say just one thing, not just with respect to Special Education, but with reference to education in general, it would be this: good teaching can level the playing field. It is one of the very few things in a young person's life that can; I have seen it with my own eyes. You cannot necessarily intervene to immediately enhance a student's general socioeconomic status, and you may not be able to undo the ravages of neglect and abuse, but you can definitely ensure that the time spent with you, within your four walls, is as good as it can possibly be. Just by being you, and by doing the very best within the profession upon which you will now embark has the power to affect lives in a very real and profound way.

It is my very strong belief that you have an obligation to create an educational environment wherein every student is given every opportunity to reach his or her full potential. But let me add a caveat here: you need to know and feel comfortable in believing that this potential does not always have to be measured in a raw academic terms. It is my strong personal opinion that, in a philosophical sense, you should settle for nothing less, and apologize to no-one in doing so. Go make a difference.

The Graduate Seminar

Heather M. Rintoul

IT HAS BEEN SOME TIME NOW since I began teaching and facilitating graduate education seminars around issues of leadership, organizational theory/management, reflective practice, and interpersonal relations. My enthusiasm for the graduate genre continues unabated. Course participants usually arrive for our seminars seemingly appreciative of the upcoming opportunity to 'make meaning' with their colleagues. Curiously, they seem to enjoy the seminar format so much that they often indicate that they will be writing the comprehensive exam in order to take more course work! This means they are undertaking ten courses, rather than writing a Major Paper which requires only eight courses, or the Thesis route which necessitates only six completed courses. The dilemma for me as course facilitator manifests as I strongly encourage Thesis and Major Paper routes; yet all the while I acknowledge student partiality to a plethora of intriguing course work!

Graduate education affords us the opportunity to expand our field of vision, and to think seriously about the many issues confronting us on a daily basis. Our coming together gives us a block of seminar time to contemplate and discriminate among a wide variety of possibilities, potentialities, and probabilities. The significant theoretical component of graduate study is made meaningful through its application to the practices/choices of our professional/personal lives in concert with lively discussion/debate.

Consider for a moment that when I refer to 'graduate' education, the use of the collective 'we' or 'us' is quite deliberate. In my view, the graduate seminar is a voyage of analysis, deconstruction/reconstruction, questioning, and discovery that we, as scholarly travellers, journey through together. The idea around the 'we' may, in part, be why I conceptualize the term 'instructor' as somewhat troubling with its attendant, and almost Socratic idea of imparting knowledge while others listen. Coupled with its singularity, the 'I' connotation of the term 'instructor' can speak to an inherent bias that is at once both oppositional and antithetical to the kind of dynamic scholarly debate and inquiry I promote in the graduate seminar. I like to think that I don't instruct, at least, I try not to, especially around issues of content. Rather I offer, encourage, facilitate, explain, listen, learn, caution, exhort, value, debate, and even cheer on quite often, but 'instruct' only rarely. One might argue convincingly that I have already done a great deal of 'instructing' even before the seminars begin, in that I have selected one text while jettisoning others, accepting or rejecting readings for inclusion in the course pack. Such a selection process, one might charge, is inherently value-laden, indicating bias. That this argument does hold merit just underscores the motivation for suppressing, as much as possible, my own 'instructive' value-laden element in the seminars themselves.

Because scholarly debate and discussion are so important, I regard attendance at, and participation in all seminars as absolutely critical and vital to our progress together. My graduate students are course 'participants', and I do expect and anticipate that they will earnestly 'take part' in the true sense of the word 'participate.' Those who choose not to participate fully are, in my view, depriving their peers of unique perspectives around issues pertaining to the course focus and divesting themselves of interesting and exciting scholarly exchanges. On rare occasions, we encounter a potential 'chair warmer,' but most seminar members eventually cannot resist offering their thoughts when they understand that their opinions and commentary are desired and valued. My role as course facilitator is a relatively minor and unimportant one that pales in comparison with the life experiences, exchanges, and narratives that my participants offer from the front line vantage point of their professional and personal life practice. As frontline professionals, they will learn infinitely more from each other than they will from me as they exchange narratives and experiences.

Initially, graduate students may be a little surprised to learn that not only are passionate curiosity, scholarly debate, agreement, disagreement, and thoughtful questioning wanted and encouraged, but they are also highly valued as a critical aspect of our progress together. For my part, I request their commitment to the course focus and a willingness to analyze, reconstruct, modify and adjust their own frameworks and visions.

Cheerfully and readily, I admit that many issues continue to confound me, and that making meaning through the connections of theory and practice is a dynamic and reflective process. Let me paraphrase Paulo Freire who, quoted elsewhere, perhaps said it best: *critical reflection on practice is a requirement of the relationship between theory and practice, otherwise theory becomes simple "blah, blah, blah" and practice, pure activism*. It seems reasonable to anticipate that in our time together, course participants will be inspired to develop their own critical perspectives about the topics and theories in and around the course focus, as well as the support for those views and the meaning they 'make' when linked to their practice. My task is to facilitate that process.

Available scholarly writings in our many areas of study are numerous. Therefore, I make a broad range of perspectives available for student perusal via articles and multi-authored texts. I anticipate that seminar participants will read critically, analyze, and deconstruct these readings to expand their field of vision, weighing issues of social and economic structure, culture and politics to inform their professional life practice.

Participants bring their own set of life experiences, opinions and beliefs to the seminars; that enriches our learning and fosters self-discovery, for while they evaluate, ponder, and debate, they often discover something new and intriguing about themselves and the world around them. The search for meaning through analysis, debate, and deconstruction may just produce that gem that resonates for that special 'ah, hah,' factor of personal and professional illumination.

Usually each participant has an opportunity to lead at least one (RRD) Reading Response and Discussion (never a summary!) around one of the course articles. Participants are encouraged to be as creative as possible, while identifying areas of agreement, disagreement and questioning, with the salient questions for discussion articulated as a hand-out. I anticipate that this experience (which is not professor-driven) will help to foster ownership of course content as each participant has the opportunity to be centre stage (if desired), and to rally the discussion around issues that resonate, and 'make meaning' for her/him. Although articles are never summarized, certainly we can and often do clarify, explain, and extrapolate just how the author's message might be interpreted. Such interpretation is a common result of cohort discussion.

The customary practice in my seminars is to request a praxis paper as the scholarly conclusion of our time together. In this paper, educational theory and practice typically come together to analyze and critically examine some problem or situation familiar to the student. The intention is for participants to have the opportunity to focus on one issue in the course, to relate it to their personal or professional experience, and to give support and justifications for their views. For this culminating task, participants are expected to draw both on course readings and other sources that are pertinent to their specified area of interest.

Then, of course, there is the lively discussion around paper evaluation. Ultimately, praxis paper evaluation is based on the rigour of the paper, that is, its organization, the extent of the analysis/reflection, and the strength and coherence of the argument/debate/discussion.

Near the conclusion of our final seminar, participants discuss the main focus of their praxis papers with their cohort. Often the cohort, wanting copies of papers, will set up an e-mail 'tree' so that everyone can access a copy of as many of the cohort papers as they wish. This enthusiasm for each others' written thoughts does not always happen, but neither is it a rarity.

As I watch and observe the excitement of the final minutes, I realize it is the participants who make the journey worthwhile, and my mental meanderings leap ahead in eager anticipation of the next cohort. The journey will begin again.

Classroom Management: A Recumbent View

Thomas G. Ryan

In my classes, my beliefs are deliberately exposed. I attempt to lead students to conclude that my understanding of classroom management is not limited to a classroom or a rigid stance, but it is a flexible disposition that I embrace and work to maintain, to modify and to evaluate each day. I believe all teachers aware of this must make efforts to reach beyond their grasp, to attend to the needs of not only the student, but also the community. Indeed, a classroom reflects the larger community. A goal in our classroom management course is to illuminate the purpose of education. I believe the purpose of education is to nurture and prepare students to become caring and responsible members of society. This citizenship emphasis means that all teachers must be able to address not only the curricula (content) but also the curriculum (whole person in the community).

The informed teaching of citizenship addresses social skills, morals, and values. However, this realization places an even larger burden on all educators. My own research has shown that the greatest threat to teacher success is the lack of time to put into practice what each teacher plans to undertake in theory. I explain to my students that one approach or solution is to become more efficient, proactive, and aware of how to achieve these ends given the obstacles of time, facilities, and number of students per class. In our classroom management class, I reflect on the lessons I have learned, I recall the ways in which I became efficient and proactive in order to pass on my wisdom, insights, and philosophy. My stories are practical lessons that are universally applicable. I recall how I handled a student who verbally abused me. I suggest ways to frame this event in order to help both the student and myself cope with the emotional injuries sustained. It is critical that educators move through times of turbulence and tension with poise and understanding.

We examine classroom management as something undertaken in a systematic and strategic manner. Our communication strategies and human systems are of pivotal importance in education. Educators use human communication channels, the non-verbal and the verbal, usually in that order, constantly. Communication theorists have argued that our communication actions are largely non-verbal (80-90%). We practice using our communication abilities in class as preservice teachers, we 'give the eye' to one another or motion for quiet during whole class dramatizations. I regularly ask students to learn more about management and themselves via role-play and case study discussions. Classroom practice involves the use of a specific intervention in order to be able to modify observed behavior. The outcome of this exercise causes students to use new language, terms, words and phrases such as token economy, response/cost, contracting, pre-correction, the turtle technique, self-management, behavioral self-control, cognitive modelling, the timer game, and so forth. Armed with new knowledge, students are eager to apply certain techniques during a practicum. The opportunity to discuss and debate our philosophical positions brings about clarity, and it is rewarding when I hear a student speak about a positive experience they had during a practicum. Conversely, I sometimes hear students who have quickly become fearful of classroom management due to a challenging practicum.

Hearing about the challenging practicum and the eventual discussion of the same causes me to remind students that educators must deal with at least two realities at the classroom level, and that they need to take time to reflect upon and revise their approach. One omnipresent reality resides in the fact that all educators must address *dilemmas*. *Dilemmas* require coping strategies in the form of individual pupil plans that are program specific and offer unique curriculum (community) supports. As well, *dilemmas* are often formally identified via an Individual Placement and Review Committee (IPRC). *Dilemmas* are school team concerns, as an identified student can have a social worker, child development counsellor, psychologist, and a teaching assistant providing support and insight.

Alternatively, educators deal with *problems*. A *problem* could be particular student behavior, for example, one who refuses to work (contrary). Usually this student can be approached and convinced to complete the work, or at least be less contrary. *Problems* are solvable, whereas *dilemmas* are situations requiring coping mechanisms. I illuminate the area of special education by describing my successes and my frustrations as IPRC labels sometimes cause more problems if we choose to look only at the label and not at the person as we guide and support them. Having a means to frame presented issues provides useful mindsets for new and experienced educators.

My students gradually come to appreciate that discipline or '*disciplino*' (the Latin root) actually means to instruct. It is from this orientation that I encourage preservice teachers to use a variety of instructional approaches in order to bring out the best in students. A multiple-intelligences approach to the curricula means that each student will have the opportunity to learn in a manner that engages their specific intelligence(s). For example, the science lesson becomes an opportunity for some students to use their artistic abilities, and for other students to see science as a way to use their oral abilities in a small group presentation. The engaged student who is able to succeed causes positive energy to amass, and this becomes a motivational force pervading not only your class but also the larger community. Success displaces anger and resentment. Hence, teachers are happy, and parents are content.

Parents are partners in education. They are essential players, and most want current information on a consistent basis. I provide my preservice students with exemplary newsletters that I have created, and I show my phone log. On my phone log, I have sunshine calls marked with happy faces, and I use other codes for other types of calls. My classes are filled with constructivist philosophy as I attempt to 'activate' previous learning in each of my students, and I guide them to use my scaffolding to construct new understandings (knowledge) which is supported by their own previous learning. I find that my approach is compatible with many cultural groups, and meets the needs I see in my classes; after all, what I am on a daily basis is more important than what I teach.

My students hear me talk about getting to know yourself as a teacher, your limitations, your standards, your vulnerabilities. I put forward the notion that it is important to have a personal life (space) that is private, a professional life that is open and healthy, and at all times, be aware of your political life. Being a professional educator is exciting, yet it carries with it professional, political, and personal responsibilities. In order to add context, the class becomes involved in scenarios that provoke thought and cause concern. Our lively debates expose positions that are often adjusted by reflection and dialog. Students realize that boundaries are required, as is self-discipline (appropriateness), and positive, rational self-talk. I challenge my students to become a student of their students.

Empowering students is a positive endeavour. It is not a matter of herding students into neat rows or looking for rule infractions. It is about establishing an environment that supports learning and in fact, most of your efforts are directed towards the maintenance of that healthy learning environment. Being a teacher who can take the pulse of the class will enable that teacher to precisely prompt a student, or ignore activities when necessary. We teach and we coach. Coaching students is not entirely a science; however, some may want to argue that it is. I believe coaching and teaching are in part artistic efforts that require informed practice, critical reflection, and constant revision throughout each educator's career.

When my last class ends, I look towards the empty seats and I reflect on the things that once were. I ask myself, "Did I miss anything?" My answer is yes, because I cannot take all of my knowledge, skill and experience and simply pass this on. Instead, I hope that each preservice (student) teacher now has an opportunity to further his or her education via experience as a full-time educator. I believe that theory informs practice and their practice infuses the theory they have embraced in our Faculty of

Education classes. It is my hope that all of our education students will establish and maintain healthy classroom environments in which all students are equal and happy members. Eventually their students will become good citizens, and if this is an outcome, then I have done my part in this cycle. I leave the empty class, only to return next term full of hope, energy, and optimism as I begin the cycle again.

The Production of Scientists, or Maybe Teachers of Science

Jeff Scott

As a child and young adult, I had always perceived the pursuit of science knowledge and skill as a passive activity: read a page from the textbook or hand-out and then answer questions, listen to the teacher talk about a science concept and then copy the notes off the board, watch a demonstration and then answer questions or complete another type of write-up. Occasionally there was an experiment to be completed, but everyone knew there was one achievable answer or solution as we were all following the same procedures while using the same materials. At no time did I feel like a '*scientist*' or someone that was encouraged to participate actively in the pursuit of science knowledge. It was apparent that this passive view of acquiring science knowledge and skills was to get to know the facts, laws, and theories associated with natural and physical phenomena. Maybe this is why I was unsuccessful in my grade 13 Chemistry course; following the term work and final exam, my mark was a 49%. After what I felt was a persuasive discussion with my teacher, my mark remained a 49%; he didn't buy the fact that I would never use science in my life, and therefore didn't feel compelled to alter my grade. I was not motivated to learn the facts, laws, and theories associated with this course, as I was a passive participant expected to 'soak up the information' and regurgitate it for a test or exam.

It wasn't until later, during my university years, that learning about science took a new direction. It was during this period that I was encouraged to ask questions, engage in interesting hands-on opportunities where procedures and the necessary equipment was determined after discussion of the question or problem, rather than procedures just being laid on and the equipment provided. It was at this time I was encouraged to participate in critical discussions in order to make sense of what I was observing based on what was occurring; rather than having someone tell me the answer, I was given the opportunity to '*discover*' for myself. For me, this is when science actually came alive! This newfound enlightenment provided me with a new interest in science, one that has provided me with a foundation for teaching science as I do. I now view science as more than acquiring a body of knowledge, or facts, to be learned, remembered, and repeated later on a test; to me this passive '*knowing*' of facts, laws, and theories associated with natural and physical phenomena is a noun rather than what it should be, a verb where one actively pursues the learning of science.

For me, as a professor of science in a Faculty of Education, it is important that my students view, engage, and learn to teach science differently than I did as a child and young adult: they must become involved with the material, they must actively investigate concepts and themes which includes experimenting, asking questions, hypothesizing, measuring, inferring, controlling variables, and communicating while utilizing a critical and problem-solving based approach. I believe the students must see science as an action, where they construct knowledge rather than just memorize it. I wish my students to understand the importance of '*sciencing*' which alters the perception of how we learn facts, concepts, laws, and theories related to science. To encourage this philosophy, I ensure that the preservice students are provided with hands-on experiences that build on the introduced teaching style or concept. I believe that the students will internalize the introduced material more efficiently by '*doing it*' rather than merely '*listening to it*'. One example presented to my students that encourages this hands-on philosophy is the learning about various forms of energy (i.e. mechanical, potential, kinetic energy), where they utilize catapults to launch 'cats' from one pad to another. As the students engage in the activity, they experiment with direction, height, and force the catapult while discussing the results of their manipulations to the catapult and the various forms of energy experienced. Connections with the intended learning, energy, are made through inquiry, discussion, as well as guided conversations between myself and the students. For me, ensuring the students understand the forms of energy and their implication in real life is important. More importantly though is the importance of providing hands-on opportunities that allows students to engage in '*sciencing*' in order to develop **A**ttitude, **S**kills, and **K**nowledge (The **A.S.K.** principle) which is the foremost tenet that I attempt to achieve in my science program.

The vast majority of the preservice teachers that initially enter my classroom are filled with anxiety, apprehension and in many cases, dread. Through stories shared with their peers, they relate their own science-based experiences, many which reflect my younger science days. They speak about the reading and answering questions, copying copious amounts of notes from the board, listening to the teacher talk about science, watching a demonstration and not being able to do it themselves, and completing an experiment by following the pre-determined path and arriving with the pre-determined conclusion. In some cases, the students speak about remembering very little about their science experiences. I believe many of these experiences have shaped how they view the learning of science.

A second tenet that I wish the students to leave my class with is attitude, that is, developing a positive attitude to science which I hope would be integrated into their underlying philosophy towards teaching and learning. If one has a positive attitude towards the material to be taught and their ability to teach it, one would hope it would be delivered in a more interesting and interactive fashion. Providing opportunities for hands-on experiences is one mode utilized to create a positive teaching/learning attitude towards science. Another key method of changing and/or creating a positive attitude is through demonstrations, specifically, discrepant events: an event that generally surprises, startles, puzzles, or astonishes the observer. The outcome of a discrepant event is often unexpected or contrary to what one would have predicted, hopefully forcing one to stimulate their natural curiosity. The event is intended to cause cognitive disequilibrium, generally pushing the observer to ask '*why?*' thus providing an impetus to become interested or motivated to seek the answer.

Other methods designed to encourage the development of a positive attitude towards teaching science includes the sharing of personal anecdotes and works of fiction and non-fiction stories. Students both young and old love to know about their teacher. Therefore when a teacher tells a personal anecdote, the student generally listens carefully. From my perspective, it is best when the story contains an interesting science/technology mystery or explanation that ties in to the concept being introduced.

Personally, one anecdote that has worked well at engaging the preservice teacher includes "a teacher, explaining to his students, that an egg, when dropped from a height, and lands on an end, will not break due to the design of the egg." I use this story to introduce the Egg Drop activity where my students utilize a technology design and everyday material such as foam, popcorn, balloons, foam pads, and small cardboard boxes to build structures that will maintain the integrity of an egg when dropped fifteen meters. Students are naturally drawn into the story, and when questioned about strength of an egg and methods for protecting the egg from breaking, the ideas are generally detailed and elaborate.

Another story I use to stimulate curiosity and provide an entry to an experiment is that of the missing data projector. The students are introduced to an activity through a story that maintains that four youth were filmed removing a data projector from the university while leaving behind a '*mystery*' powder; it is up to the preservice students to determine who the culprit is by analyzing various powders that was reportedly left by one of the culprits.

It has been written that all teachers worthy of the name are creative and gifted storytellers. I believe that it is often through stories that we are best able to share with learners the vitality and relevance of our knowledge. An anecdote with good humor and/or novelty, which relates to the underlying scientific or technological concept, tends to spawn memorable moments. Meanwhile, reading stories, both fiction and non-fiction, also have the ability to pique the imagination and supply information while providing opportunities for asking questions and seeking answers, again providing a method for developing a positive attitude. The sharing of a personal anecdote or fiction or non-fiction story is often a daily classroom experience.

In the Primary/Junior classroom, I feel that one must approach teaching the science and technology curricula not as a stand-alone subject, but one that can be integrated into other areas including math, social studies, language arts, drama, art, music, and physical education. This is the third tenet I wish my students to leave my course with. Many of the basic science concepts can be approached in an integrated fashion. For example, when learning about medieval weaponry in the social studies curricula, which employed levers, pulleys and gears, one can integrate the learning into the science, language, mathematics, and information technology curricula. Students can explore basic catapult design by accessing the material on the internet, utilize mathematical concepts for measuring both lengths of pieces when creating the catapult as well as the distance the projectile travels and language for reading about catapults as well as writing up the findings. Other opportunities for integrating science concepts into additional curricula areas include the employment of transactional writing which can be utilized to capture what has been learned about Animals, the Human Body, or Space topics, all of which are studied at various grades.

It is the creative, well planned, and organized teacher that can implement the science curriculum in an authentic and meaningful manner, one that provides for and encourages hands-on activities, creative thinking, and problem solving through an integrated approach. With this approach, one would expect to foster the development of a positive **A**ttitude, a set of **S**kills including guessing/predicting/hypothesizing, experimenting, seriating, measuring, communicating while developing **K**nowledge; and it is this teacher, utilizing this approach that I wish to see leaving my classroom, maybe not as a scientist, but as a teacher of science!

Preaching What I Practiced: From Practitioner to Professor

Maria Cantalini-Williams

My earliest recollections of my desire to be a teacher stems from a short essay that I wrote in grade six entitled (of course), "What I Want to Be When I Grow Up." I distinctly remember writing that I wanted to be a grade two teacher, because in grade one there was the awesome responsibility of teaching students to read, and in grade three, children had to be taught cursive writing, therefore I thought that grade two would be just an interesting year without particular challenges. As what may have been expected of a daughter of Italian immigrants, I was encouraged to pursue higher education, but my parents only knew of three careers from which to choose: secretary, nurse, or teacher. And thus I chose to be a teacher, and followed that dream by becoming a classroom teacher, followed by a consultant for teachers, and now as a teacher of student teachers.

It is in my present role as an assistant professor, for courses such as Curriculum Methods and Education and Schooling, that I am articulating for my students that which I experienced as a teacher and consultant, meshed with my theoretical knowledge of the field.

My philosophy on life has changed from wanting to teach a 'comfortable' grade to now actively seeking new challenges and stimulation, but my love for education and learning has remained constant. I did actually teach grade one and two for my first years of teaching, and most often taught in the primary division in each of my teaching assignments. In these teaching situations, I learned much about young children, families, the teaching profession, and the development of lifelong learning. From walking in the shoes of a teacher, I was able to not only put into practice the teachings and understandings gleaned from my teacher education at the Institute of Child Study in Toronto, but also to integrate my own personal beliefs about the learning process. It is this learning that I now 'talk' or 'preach' about in my classes.

In my courses, I have the privilege of espousing my thoughts, reflections and observations from my years as a teacher, a graduate of doctoral studies, and a consultant. In addition, I have been an active parent in public schooling, and my husband is an elementary school principal. My stories abound from my experiences and the anecdotes hopefully make the classes more meaningful and interesting. The topics addressed in these classes mirror the topics of concern to both today's and yesterday's teachers. In the course, Curriculum Methods, we address the development of the learner, the various learning styles, planning, teaching strategies, assessment and parental involvement among other topics. In my past roles as teacher and program consultant, I either attended and/or delivered several hundred workshops, courses, institutes, seminars, in-services, presentations and more on these topics. I walked the road of curriculum review, development and implementation in various grades and subject areas.

The main messages that I offer in the Methods course are: knowledge of the children's backgrounds and interests as influences in planning for the class; assessment precedes instruction; teachers teach children, not a grade; parents deserve to know everything about your class; children are inherently good; all children can learn, just not in the same way and on the same day; and if a lesson fails or a child fails, ask yourself "why?" and try different strategies, and never give up on a class or on a child. It is the teacher's responsibility to engage all children and to help them to develop and grow in each area of learning.

I often repeat that based on my experiences, all learning is on a continuum, and we need to be able to prove (demonstrate or provide evidence) that children have grown, developed, and thrived in our class. I use an analogy from medicine. Parents ask doctors two questions at each check-up visit: "How much has my child grown (in height and weight) since the last check-up?" and "How does my child compare with other children of a similar age?" In school, we should be able to answer those same questions: "How has this child developed and learned in my class?" and "How does this child compare to standards/norms for this grade?" I also inform my students that we need to be aware that school curriculum standards were not necessarily based on a "norm" from a cross-section of students, and that they are grade-based and not age-based as would be more developmentally appropriate. We have many discussions about the validity of the sets of curriculum expectations that teachers are expected to 'cover' instead of 'discover, uncover, or recover.'

My students reminisce about the days when they helped to determine the 'themes' for the curriculum of the class and the days that they manipulated the sand, water, blocks and paint easels in meaningful experiences, as was my experience as a teacher during the 'whole language days'. We question why 'experts' say that whole language did not work when they are the successful graduates of the school system.

The students point out to me that literacy is overdone in today's schools, and that the children seem to be 'turned off' in some classes due to an absence of the arts and other subjects. We debate, discuss and negotiate the curriculum of our own course in an effort to find a balance between teacher and student directed learning. Most notably, I have taught the lesson on "lesson planning" by using the Nipissing template for lesson planning (the same plan my students are expected to use) as my guide. I strive to be authentic in my interactions, in my teaching and particularly in the assessment of my students in an effort to preach what I practiced but also to practice what I preach.

In the Education and Schooling course, we explore such topics as the image of the teacher in society, the professional standards of teaching, educational law, philosophies of education, history of education and societal issues in education. This course lends itself to introspection and a careful dissection of the present system of schooling. We question our own motives for having become teachers, society's expectations of teachers, the media's portrayal of teachers through movies, television shows, and the stories in newspapers or magazines, and even in children's literature. I practice what I preach by beginning each class with an excerpt from a children's book or novel that depicts teachers or schooling. I am also talking the walk because I believe that reading aloud is a very important component of each student's school experience across the grades. Through books such as *Loser*, *Anne of Avonlea*, or even *Franklin Goes to School*, we discern messages about what society believes school to be. Themes of report cards, achievement, bullying, and parental involvement are all evident in these books about 'education and schooling'.

In examining historical changes in education, I show my students samples of textbooks and ministry guidelines from the mid-1900s (some are my own primary workbooks), and we determine what is different from, but also the same as what is in today's classrooms. While addressing laws in education, we reflect on the philosophies that may have provided the basis for such laws as the Safe Schools Act. It is interesting to note that the philosophers of yesteryear (for example, John Dewey) are still talked about in schools of education if not followed in today's schools. My students are developing their own philosophies of education, just as I was asked to do in my own assignments in teacher preservice and graduate courses. The Education and Schooling course provides a foundation for teacher candidates, and further learning will hopefully build on this solid base of understanding about how schools evolved from the past and operate presently.

In closing, I feel privileged to have the opportunity to share my past experiences with tomorrow's teachers. In a faculty of education, we are truly functioning in 'teaching schools.' We are helping student teachers assimilate their own schooling experiences with those they observe in practicum, in conjunction with the theories with which they are becoming familiar through courses and readings. The students are acclimatizing to the new learning, and developing new schema about the meaning of teaching. It is my hope that graduates of teacher education programs continually observe, ask questions, seek solutions, and strive to improve education as a lifelong quest. I hope that, as a student of life, love, laughter, and learning, I model this quest.

Afterword

Each of the preceding contributions, regardless of form or discipline, has at its foundation, an abiding passion for teaching and the understanding of the profound importance of reflective practice. Collectively they speak, with honesty, of the challenges and joys of maintaining the all important balance, so vital to teacher education, between theory and practice. Taken for granted within these stories are the acquired years of practical experience in schools, the ongoing personal and professional research and writing, the need for content and curriculum understanding, and the demands of ever changing Ministerial policy. Though not explicitly stated, these too play their part in the balancing act experienced daily by teacher educators. Despite this, the theme most common to these stories is the belief that the individual teacher stands at the heart of education, with the capacity to influence the life trajectory of each one of their individual students. As is apparent in these stories, for these educators, there is so greater joy or responsibility than this.

About the Authors

Dr. Warnie Richardson *is an Associate Professor of Special Education and Educational Psychology at Nipissing University in Northern Ontario, Canada. Prior to arriving at Nipissing University, Dr. Richardson was a Special Education teacher/ Educational Assessor for sixteen years, all in very hard to serve educational environments in Canada and the Caribbean. His doctoral work at the University of Toronto and most of his writing to date has focused on the schooling experience of juvenile delinquents and the resiliency of marginalized or youth at risk.*

Dr. Carole Richardson *is an Assistant Professor of Curriculum Studies in Music Education in the Faculty of Education at Nipissing University in Northern Ontario, Canada. Prior to arriving at Nippising University, Dr. Richardson taught general classroom music and conducted choirs in both primary and middle schools in Ontario and the Cayman Islands. Her narrative research focuses on the importance of Arts experiences in the lives of her students and their students. She is a continuous advocate for and promoter of the importance of student engagement in positive and authentic musical experiences, and currently teaches general music methods to Junior/Intermediate preservice teachers.*